Tailings

Tailings

a memoir

Kaethe Schwehn

▲ CASCADE *Books* · Eugene, Oregon

TAILINGS
A Memoir

Cascade Books
An Imprint of Wipf and Stock Publishers
199 W. 8th Ave., Suite 3
Eugene, OR 97401

www.wipfandstock.com

ISBN 13: 978-1-62564-562-3

Cataloguing-in-Publication Data

Schwehn, Kaethe.

Tailings : a memoir / Kaethe Schwehn.

xii + 124 p. ; 23 cm.

ISBN 13: 978-1-62564-562-3

1. Communal living—Washington State. 2. Christian communities. I. Title.

BX7615 .S5 2014

Manufactured in the U.S.A.   10/07/2014

"Four Poems for Robin" by Gary Snyder, from THE BACK COUNTRY, copyright
©1968 by Gary Snyder. Reprinted by permission of New Directions Publishing Corp.

"Nada Te Turbe / Nothing Can Trouble" by Taizé. Copyright © 1986, Ateliers et Presses
de Taizé, Taizé Community, France GIA Publications, Inc., exclusive North American
agent 7404 S. Mason Ave., Chicago, IL 60638 www.giamusic.com 800.442.1358 All
rights reserved. Used by permission.

"Take, O Take Me As I Am" by John L. Bell. Copyright © 1995, Wild Goose Resource
Group, Iona Community, Scotland GIA Publications, Inc., exclusive North American
agent 7404 S. Mason Ave., Chicago, IL 60638 www.giamusic.com 800.442.1358 All
rights reserved. Used by permission.

Tony Hoagland, excerpts from "Adam and Eve" from Donkey Gospel. Copyright ©
1998 by Tony Hoagland. Reprinted with the permission of The Permissions Company,
Inc., on behalf of Graywolf Press, Minneapolis, Minnesota, www.graywolfpress.org.

"Tailings," an essay based on portions of this memoir, was published in *Witness Magazine* (Spring, 2013).

for
my parents

for
the Holden Village Winter Community
2001–2002

in memory of
Bethany Hartung
1985–2007

"May the spirit of God disturb you."

Gertrude Lundholm

Contents

Author's Note

One summer a sign posted to greet visitors as they entered Holden Village carried this message: "You're not the same as when you came. Neither are we." Holden Village, though firmly rooted in the Gospels and dedicated to values like community, justice, hilarity, and hospitality, is also a place of constant flux. This memoir is an attempt to reconstruct a particular place at a particular moment in time. Those who love Holden will find moments of familiarity and deep recognition here, but it's also true that those who claim the village as home might find some details to be foreign or incongruous, discordant with their own notion of the place. Thus, this book is also invitation; to arrive at a whole understanding of Holden Village, many more stories need to be told. Lola Deane's edited collection *Holden Village: 50 Years of Memories* is a wonderful beginning. I hope there will be many more such additions. I am not a spokesperson for Holden Village, but I have been a person changed, over and over again, by my time there.

This book is a work of memory. For the sake of clarity, a few of the characters are composites and a few of the names have been changed.

Acknowledgments

It takes a community to write a book.

Ricki Thompson and Mark Schwehn were incredibly supportive and in-sightful about these pages, even when the content put them in vulnerable positions. I am so grateful.

In addition to her careful attention to these words, my mother often paid very careful attention to my children, Thisbe and Matteus, so that I could pay attention to these words. Thanks, Mom.

The Loft Mentor Series and the Minnesota State Arts Board provided im-portant literary and financial support during the writing of the manuscript. Thanks to Jared Santek and the other Loft Mentees.

I'm grateful to the writers who read early and later drafts of this manu-script: John Hildebrand, Dinty Moore, Tami Mohammed Brown, Lynne Maker Kuechle, Liza Allen, Jan Hill, Diane LeBlanc, Mary Winstead, Jenny Dunning. And the Supergroupers: Kate Schultz, Jana Hiller, Coralee Grebe, Sean Beggs, Sarah Hanley, and Kristi Belcamino. Christian Scharen is owed a pie for helping me find Cascade Books; Martha and Sam Bardwell and John and Anna Rohde Schwehn deserve badges of honor for endless

Acknowledgments

conversations about titles. Thank you also to Anjali Sachdeva, Adam Go-
laski, Kiki Petrosino, and Kim Brooks for providing emotional support and
wine at key moments in the creative process. René Steinke, Todd Boss, and
Tom Montgomery Fate offered wisdom and advice. Thank you to Dorothy
Bass and Peter Thompson for loving me from the (almost) very beginning.

My thanks also to those who provided information, insight, and anecdotes
about Holden's history, geology, and cultural artifacts: Wrick Dunning,
DeAne Lagerquist, Linda Jensen, Tom Witt, Carol Hinderlie, Janet Grant,
Magdalena Briehl Wells, and dozens of Holden friends on Facebook who
responded to requests for information both bizarre and mundane.

I'm incredibly grateful to the Holden community at large and the winter
community of 2001–2002 specifically for always providing a home on the
journey. This portion of the Acknowledgements, like the reading of the arrivals list at a Holden summer Vespers, could go on forever. Those who are
not named here are certainly named in my heart. Specifically, a few of the
former twenty-somethings: Miriam Schmidt, Jeremy Blyth, Kent Gustav-
son, Kent Narum, Aaron Greig, Aaron Nelson, Kristian Bentsen, Heather
Spears, Jamie Ponce, Kris Hendrickson, Mark Genszler, Adam Gaede, and
Jeshua Erickson. Thanks to S. S., who returned my letters because he knew
I might need to write this story someday. Thanks to James Stutrud and
to Tuque, the village mascot. And to Michael Thompson, *el regalo más
hermoso*.

And finally, my deepest gratitude goes to Peder Jothen; my life with you is
far better than anything my twenty-two-year-old self could have intended.

SEPTEMBER

Nine Switchbacks

There is only one road to the village. The road begins at a lake whose cold is a firecracker to the chest. The road doesn't linger at the lake, the road goes groping up the mountain. Nine switchbacks and the road gets dizzy with the sway, needs to catch a breath, goes straight and narrow for eight miles, past a few halfhearted waterfalls, past alumroot and chicory, past lodgepole pine and silver fir. When the road comes to the village it stutters for three hundred yards, between chalets and lodges, between mess hall and gymnasium. Just past the village the forest begins to encroach on the road, pine needles underfoot instead of dust and rock until, one mile later, the road sputters out in a field of grass and ground squirrel dens. The village used to be a mining village; now it is a Lutheran retreat center.

In the summertime retired pastors and young families come to this village in central Washington to attend classes and weave rugs and hike to waterfalls and sip coffee in adirondack chairs. They gulp deep breaths of mountain air and celebrate the lack of phones and television reception and Internet access. In the winter the village is kept alive by sixty-five people who are in some state of transition in their lives; they are between jobs or relationships or identities. They are vehemently Christian or vehemently not. Over the course of the upcoming winter these villagers will laugh and fight and eat and screw. They will discuss Bonhoeffer and brew beer and paint silk scarves. They will make earrings out of mine debris and toboggan down Chalet Hill with whiskey still slick on their tongues. One villager will come out of the closet. One will take a vow of silence and one will contemplate statutory rape. One will break her pelvis and one will crack his wrist. One will fear her child is being molested and one will miscarry twice. Some villagers will fall in love and some will fall out of love and a handful will contemplate suicide. Over the course of the winter, 354 inches of snow will fall. The people will pray for transformation while the copper tailings stain the creek.

I am the teaching assistant at the school in the village. But I didn't come to the village to teach, I came because I was a teacher and I want to be a writer and the village is a place to live when you are between two parts of your life. I left my teaching but I also left behind a man, a lover, a paramour, a partner, an Intended. I am between the part of my life that included my Intended and the part that will not. Generally the world divides time into before and after, this job and then that one. The village provides a liminal space, a way of dwelling deliberately in the unknown.

My parents didn't know this when they came to the village for the first time in 1980. They thought they were coming to enjoy the adventure of the wilderness, the fellowship of Christian community. They didn't realize they were inhabiting the tender space between eleven years of marriage and thirty-plus years of divorce.

J. H. Holden didn't know this when he arrived in 1896, before the village was a village, when it was just valley and mountain. Holden wanted a quick before and after: rock to copper, mountain to mine, rags to riches. But although he discovered the vein of copper, he lived through twenty-two years of leases and assessments. Holden never saw the mine become operational, didn't live to see the place named Holden Village in honor of his discovery. He spent two decades of his life waiting for the future he intended.

I spend my days in the three-room schoolhouse, completed in 1938, twenty years after Holden died. This year, the school consists of twelve students: seven high school students and five elementary students. On this particular morning, the third day of school, I am sitting on a couch in the high school room, watching the teacher draw two vertical rectangles on the chalkboard. "They were like this," he says. Then he erases the upper edge of one of the rectangles and the sides until it is only an eighth of the height of the rectangle beside it. He redraws the upper edge. "Now the tower is like this."

It is September 11, 2001 and we have no television reception. There is the world before September 11 and the world after September 11th. We will spend the next year living somewhere in between.

There are three ways out of the village. The first is via helicopter. If you break your neck in an avalanche (2000) or fall off a cliff and into a raging creek (1996) or suffer a severe allergic reaction after eating a bite of not-actually-dairy-free lasagna (1997), you can be airlifted out. If there isn't fog in the valley, if there is enough light and the winds are relatively still, the helicopter will land on a pile of copper tailings on the other side of Railroad Creek.

Most people leave the village by the taking the road down the valley to Lake Chelan. Once you reach Lake Chelan you have to wait for a boat to take you down lake. In the summer the boat ride will take three hours. In the winter a faster boat is used but you have to catch it on its way up lake and then ride it all the way back down. In December, the time from the village to a store that sells tortillas and peanut butter and sponges is approximately six hours.

The third way out is to hike in the other direction, up valley instead of down. After two miles you'll come to a series of footbridges so carefully built into the trail that you might not notice them until you hear the hollow sound under your feet. In another mile you'll come to a trailhead. If you go right you'll climb the switchbacks to Holden Lake. If you stay to the left you can go to Hart Lake. Lyman Lake. Cloudy Pass. From the pass you can see three valleys if you can see at all. If the wind is moving fast enough, the clouds will roll directly over the spine of the pass and you will pull your Gortex hood up and turn your face to the right so your lover can see how the wind is burning your cheeks. If there is no wind, you can be socked in for hours or days. From Cloudy Pass, you can wend your way to Stehekin, the town at the furthest tip of Lake Chelan, via Agnes Creek. Or you can follow the sloping mountain meadow to Image Lake, eat hummus and pita at a fire lookout tower, and then amble the next twenty miles to a civilized town.

This is a lie. There are a million ways out of the mountains.

OCTOBER

Fortune Teller Fish

My Intended is supposed to return in October. Is supposed to bring my stereo and my snowshoes, partly because I need these things and partly because, though we have decided to take a break, a separation never sticks until one of the parties falls in love with someone else. So a part of me has an eye on the mailboxes, on the bus arrivals. A part of me is always looking for a sign of his return.

Today is Transition Day, the day we transform the village from a large summer retreat center to a small winter community. In the summer we house over 450 people on any given day; in the winter, even when the village swells beyond its usual number with January-term college students or weekend retreaters, our numbers rarely exceed one hundred. So we have to prepare the buildings for hibernation, need to clean and flip and store, need to gird ourselves for the onslaught of snow and the impending darkness. It's the day we hunker down and truly examine who it is we'll be living beside for the next nine months.

We're scheduled to break up into work crews at 8:30 so by 8:00 the dining hall is filled with most of the villagers. My family, one side of my family, is in the village too. I spot my mother over by the oversized coffee urns and my stepfather, Peter, ladling oatmeal out of a silver tureen. My brother, Michael, is standing by the industrial sized toaster, hypnotically transfixed by the sight of the bread slowly moving down the grated

4

conveyor belt. I poke my mom in the butt and she swats at my hand. I love my family but I don't love the fact that I'm twenty-two years old and living in a remote mountain village with them. The original plan was to spend the year here with the Intended. When my parents expressed interest in coming along too, it somehow seemed not-too-weird; I would have my life with the Intended and they could live their lives beside us. But now that I'm here by myself, the whole arrangement feels mildly humiliating.

I skip the coffee urns and head directly to the silver counter. The counter lines the north end of the dining hall; the work of the kitchen goes on behind it. Lucas stirs oatmeal in a huge silver bowl while Miriam kneads bread on the counter.

"Press pot?" I say.

Lucas peels off his white latex gloves and hands me the pot. "Second one of the morning. Still warm."

Lucas is one of the few volunteer cooks who actually has experience cooking. Before coming to Holden, Lucas was the cook at a men's homeless shelter in Seattle. Unlike the other cooks in the village (trained in Holden's mostly vegetarian oeuvre), Lucas knows meat. How to baste and slice, how to grill and fry. How to cut a pork loin so it will be tender, how to cook roast beef so that it turns dark brown with a pale rose in the center instead of chalky gray. His dairy allergy is so severe that he has to leave the dining hall when the other cooks mix the powdered milk. Blue eyes, blond hair, a frame thinned by cigarettes, he wears a bandana to cook, always, and his wire-rimmed glasses. He has a professional, almost brusque manner when he's in the kitchen but when we're alone his gaze, usually rooted in the back of his skull moves outward, becomes intimate and penetrating. I take the press pot.

"We put out half and half today," adds Miriam.

Usually, my only option for softening the bitterness of the coffee is the half-powdered, half-regular milk combination that the cooks pour into silver pitchers every morning. Half and half is a luxury.

"We pull out all the stops on Transition," says Lucas, "we just go crazy."

"I might even put out whipping cream later," says Miriam.

"Things could get insane," says Lucas.

Miriam smiles, sprinkles a little more flour on the silver counter, and rips a small chunk of dough off a hulking mass that reminds me vaguely of Jabba the Hutt. She sets the dough on a scale, peers over her glasses to study the shuddering needle, and then puts the dough on the counter and digs the heels of her hands into it. The cooks bake fresh bread daily and this is what Miriam loves: not just the weighing of the dough or the kneading, not just the sprinkling of flour over the clean counter or the brushing of egg yolk on browning loaves, but talking about what it means. Ritual and practice, how coming together over food changes the lives of those involved. Last Sunday, as the assisting minister at Eucharist, Miriam's outstretched hands were graceful, the gesture of lifting prayers to God as natural as pulling a strand of hair behind her ear or pinching the bridge of her nose.

Maybe I like Miriam for how different she seems. She's a New Yorker at heart; she usually wears black, sometimes coupled with a fleece in a dim earthy tone. She has short, spiky black hair and tortoiseshell glasses. She lived the last three years in Taos, New Mexico, with a woman whose name she pronounces delicately, like tissue paper. When I'm with her I think it would be nice to have a woman float my name into space with that kind of care.

I dump half and half in my coffee, grab a piece of toast, and settle myself in a chair just as Gregory, the operations manager, arrives at the small podium in the middle of the south end of the dining hall and turns on the microphone. He explains that we'll be breaking up into different work crews, reminds us to wear close-toed shoes and to lift from the legs, and then steps back so that the crew leaders can summon their forces.

I'm on Kent's crew. Kent is actually a cook but he's tall and strong with a brooding and authoritative look that makes him an appealing team captain. In the kitchen, Kent chooses bluegrass or blues for the stereo because it's what he loves to play. Kent's voice is raspy; he sings songs about trains disappearing, about the old wheel turning, about the time not being long. He was in Palestine a few years ago, he was playing music with Palestinian and Israeli children when his friend, a Palestinian, was killed. During the summer Kent fell in love with a big-boned German woman who was volunteering in the kitchen; he's spent the weeks since her departure writing her furiously scribbled letters, sometimes in German, sometimes in English. Our job, he explains, is to tend to the objects that might be harmed or destroyed by the 300-plus inches of snow we'll likely receive over the course of the winter.

We head outside and begin by flipping the huge oak picnic table on its side; we nestle the benches close to the table's haunches. Then we collect the adirondack chairs and place them in the dingy basement of Lodge Two. We take down chalet flowerboxes and scour the rest of the village for random tools and implements; snow is predicted tomorrow and we want to salvage what we can before it goes missing for the next six months. Then Kent gives me the task of dismantling the Tree of Life.

The Tree of Life stands at the heart of the village, just to the left of a wooden platform called the Ark. Above the Ark is the bell, a remnant of the mining days, attached to a rope whose other end is slung around the railing of the dining hall. Someone pulls the rope to summon everyone to meals, Vespers, and meetings. In the summertime, kids clamor around the rope in the minutes leading up to mealtimes, hoping for the honor of getting to tip the clapper into song.

Constructed in 1999 by Sister Paula Mary Turnbull, the Tree is constructed out of pipes from the mine itself and copper manufactured out of the concentrate pulled from the mountain. In the Bible the Tree of Life appears as one of the few benevolent figures in the book of Revelation. The Tree bears twelve kinds of fruit and its leaves are intended for the healing of the nations. To a Lutheran, the idea of a Tree of Life formed out of salvaged parts feels powerful. The mine and its tailings are responsible for polluting Railroad Creek and the valley around it; how lovely to connect devastation with healing, pollution with new life. While I, too, love the idea theoretically, I don't much care for the idea in practice. The trunk and arms of the tree are formed mostly from the rusted copper piping; the dangling leaves and fruit have been pounded out of the salvaged copper and their healing potential isn't promising. The pieces are cold and make my hands smell like blood; I'm not exactly sad to be dismantling the tree. I wrap each item in a piece of newspaper and place them in a cardboard box that I seal and label "Tree of Life" in red permanent marker. When I'm finished, the trunk still stands, cemented into the ground, looking very much like it's waiting to impale someone.

I hear a grating sound and some cursing. My stepfather, Peter, and Aaron, Finn, and John are pushing a large ice cream freezer up the brick path from the road to the dining hall. In the summer the dining hall is simply used for eating. Orange rectangular tables from the mining days (as their weight and general tendency toward immobility remind us) line the south wall. More modern, less stable circular tables run down the middle of the room. Today half of the tables will be removed and replaced with a small pool table, a ping-pong table, and a foosball table. The freezer, usually housed in the Snack Bar, will be positioned between the bulk cereal dispenser and the glass tea jars so that we can enjoy scoops of rocky road and mint chocolate chip on Wednesday and Friday nights throughout the winter.

"This is going to give me a hernia," says Peter, readjusting his grip on the slick side of the freezer.

"This freezer is going to give me a hard on," says Finn, gyrating his hips into the side of perhaps the least sexual object in the entire village.

"Save it for the dining hall," says John. "You can make all the freezer babies you want when we get this up there."

"Care to give us a hand?" says Aaron.

"Nah," I say, lifting the box in my hands a little higher. "I'm already carrying the Tree of Life."

Aaron rolls his eyes.

Aaron and Peter are Operations Floaters. Basically, this means they do most of the manual labor in the village that doesn't involve shoveling snow, cutting firewood, or moving heavy objects from one place to another. Those jobs are reserved for the head Mavericks, Finn and John. The main job of the operations crew this year is to remodel Lodge One. Because Holden Village is an historic site, we have to get special permission from the Forest Service before altering the outsides of the buildings in any way. Even a fresh coat of paint in the same color requires a pile of paperwork. The insides of the buildings, however, are free game.

So Lodge One has been gutted and is currently an empty ribcage of framing boards. Electrical wires dangle from the ceilings and here and there a few space heaters choke out a bit of warmth. Though not really crass by nature, Aaron and Peter have already become more foul-mouthed as the days have grown colder. Last week, during a particular nasty cold front, the temperatures hung in the forties and Aaron and Peter began to take more frequent coffee breaks. I'd find them in the dining hall, leaning back in their chairs, ceramic cups of lukewarm coffee in front of them, talking about the size of their balls (currently no bigger than marbles) and attempting to qualify (using the Richter scale) the potency of Aaron's farts. The Mavericks and the carpenters and the operations folk all wear Carhartt jackets and Carhartt pants and knit caps and work boots. They each carry a Leatherman and a set of earplugs in their pockets; the scent of work on their bodies has become muffled as the days grow colder and the layers grow thicker.

As I trudge up the dining hall steps with the Tree of Life, Miriam comes out to ring the bell for lunch. I follow her inside and we move through the buffet line, collecting salad and slices of fresh bread and bowls of minestrone soup. The east end of the dining hall is now officially in transition. The circular tables have been laid on their sides, segmented legs tucked to chests. The space they occupied now features couches, comfy chairs, and a bookshelf, pulled from other parts of the village. On the bookshelf a green *Lutheran Book of Worship* leans against *Jurassic Park*; *Chutes and Ladders* sits next to a basket of knitting odds and ends. Before I've finished my soup, Finn and Aaron have set up the ping pong table; though I can't see them I can hear the ball tick-ticking back and forth across the net.

After lunch I'm assigned to my mother's team. She's the head housekeeper and generally spends her days scrubbing toilets and sweeping hallways and vacuuming the rugs in the communal spaces. When guests come to the village she prepares their rooms; when they leave she cleans the mirrors and squirts sanitizer in the sinks and wipes toothpaste spatter off the mirrors. When she runs out of things to do, she tackles the spots on the dining hall carpet. Just before lunch this is often where I find her, on her hands and knees, rubbing at the carpet with a dirty rag, leaning back on her heels from time to time to survey her work.

Today she's in charge of shutting down most of the guest rooms for the upcoming winter: flipping mattresses, removing linens, checking drawers and cabinets one last time for forgotten socks or Pokémon figurines or half-empty packets of beef jerky. She assigns me the task of cleaning the Venetian blinds that hang in a few of the guest rooms. For about five minutes there is a real satisfaction in scattering the dust and discovering the shine of the green or ivory vinyl below. The vinegar in my eco-friendly cleanser (mixed by hand in a closet in the basement of the dining hall) smells vibrant and Dar Williams, my chosen walkman soundtrack, is singing about Christians and pagans gathered around a table. I shake my hips and shake the dust loose. After five minutes I'm bored. After seven minutes I'm really bored. I make happy faces and hearts in the dust; I twist the rotating drum to see if reversing the direction of the blinds will make them seem cleaner. I think about how I am not particularly good at repetitive tedious tasks. I think about the miners.

From 1938–1957 the work of the village was mining. Or rather the work of the men in the village was mining. The work of the men was into the tunnels, was pickaxes and drills, was filling railway carts with what they'd blasted from the inner lung of the mountain. The men wore work boots and thick pants held up by suspenders. Faces smudged with dirt, they looked like variations on a theme. In the photos from that time, the whites of their eyes always gleam brightest. The men came to the village for the work and the work made them who they were. Like the miners, most of the twenty-somethings at Holden have come here to do work we don't necessarily love. But because we are in between moments in our lives, we assume the work will be temporary, we believe it reflects where we are rather than who we are. Work fills the present while we tackle the more daunting task of what we will do with the future.

The term *vocation* is and has been defined in lots of different ways. Around 1520 Martin Luther stole the term away from Catholics who reserved the term for monks and nuns, those who had been called to work directly in God's bosom. Luther claimed that although a Christian's true vocation was the act of serving God and the world, one didn't need to take religious vows to practice one's vocation. It was possible for any type of work to be a vocation as long as the worker was conscientious about how he or she performed that duty. By Luther's definition, the work we do in the village could indeed qualify as our vocations. But villagers lean more toward Presbyterian Frederick Buechner's definition than Luther's. Buechner also thought that vocation was about serving God but he believed that one's own talents and capabilities might be part of God's desires. Vocation, for Buechner, wasn't just about serving God through work, it was about serving God through the work that you do best, finding the place where, in his words, "your deep gladness meets the world's deep need."

Vocation, for many of us here in the village, is about discernment, about turning inward to reflect before turning outward to serve the world. Obviously, this philosophy assumes a certain amount of privilege; people who have time for introspection are often college educated, often upper-middle class, often white. Most of the twenty-somethings at Holden fall into this category. And most of us understand this year as a time of reckoning, a time of transition, a time of passing through.

Although I love teaching, my own deep gladness comes from writing. But in order to serve the world with my writing, I need to be good at it. I'm not sure that I am. I'm the teaching assistant in the village school, but every morning I show up at the dining hall an hour before school starts, open my black spiral notebook, and pull my pen across the page. In December and January I'll apply to MFA programs. Then I'll wait to see if my own gladness is deep enough to meet the world's deep need.

At the moment, my own deep need is to stop cleaning these blinds. I drop my rag in a bucket filled with dirty towels and lug the entire bucket up to the laundry. Then I head down to the dining hall cleaning closet, mix up more sanitizer, and fill spray bottle after spray bottle with it. On my way back to my room I check the mailboxes in the dining hall entryway. I told the Intended to send me an estimated arrival date as soon as he knew when he'd return. He promised October but my mailbox is empty yet again. I run my finger all the way to the back of the box, checking to be sure the wood frame doesn't open to a Narnian world of forgotten letters, before heading back to my chalet to dress for dinner.

Transition dinner is a swanky occasion. Or swanky by village standards. The meal is an occasion to dress nicely; for some people this means slacks or a skirt while others use it as an opportunity to flaunt a slinky cocktail number brought from home or use it as an excuse to visit the costume shop. "Shop" is perhaps a misleading term. The costume room, an attic-like space in the large village Center, features a single bar from which decades of dresses, uniforms, and Halloween costumes hang. Scattered around the room are milk crates filled with various accessories (shoes, wigs, purses, etc.). The room is cold, even in the summer, so most of the time villagers emerge with the first thing that fits rather than the costume item they actually hoped to find.

I forego the costume shop in favor of a dress from my deceased grandmother's collection. It's ankle-length, hugs my boobs, and features contrasting black and white geometric patterns; looking at it too long is nauseating. Jeremy and I invited a number of the twenty-somethings up to our attic suite for a cocktail hour before dinner. By "cocktails" it's understood we mean the box of red wine in my room and the bottle of whiskey in his. Our rooms are at the top of Chalet One, separated by a tiny, three-foot by three-foot hallway.

Jeremy, one of my closest confidants in the village, is the plumber, though it's clear to most of us that Jeremy knows very little about plumbing. Sinewy and muscular with a slightly rounded belly, he wears a green felt hat and a green wool sweater with moth-eaten holes in the cuffs. When there isn't a plumbing emergency he spends his days soldering pipes, nozzles, bongs. I often find Jeremy sliding his tongue along the white edge of rolling paper or tapping his foot while the single serving percolator boils or lounging in the bath, holding a sheaf of papers out of the water. He calls me his *flat mate*, his *double stacked poetessa*. His drinks scotch out of a ceramic mug. Tacked to the sloping pine ceiling of his room are black and white photographs: crevices with humans climbing up their lengths, the undercarriage of a car, the pilings of a bridge. In one photo a woman leans out over the edge of a balcony. It is night and you can see the slope of her back and also the bright lights on the street below.

I'm admiring the photos when our guests come clomping up the stairs. We distribute drinks into a creative assortment of cups: two mugs with college insignias, two camping cups, a ceramic pencil holder, and a bud vase that must be held by the owner at all times since its rounded bottom prevents an upright stance. The owners of the cups are equally haphazard: Aaron has paired rumpled slacks and shirt with a fur stole and rabbit ears from the costume shop; Finn is impeccably dressed in a baby blue suit and orange tie (his colors of choice); Lucas sports flowered green jeans (a GAP clearance item) and a matching green bandana; Miriam looks closest to normal in a clingy black shift, black boots, and silk scarf; Jeremy wears his standard felt hat but has added to his ensemble a clean t-shirt and rainbow suspenders. He's replaced the moth-eaten sweater with a sea-foam green woman's cardigan.

It's nearing time for dinner and I'm woozy from the wine in my empty stomach. We look good, this group of us. Washed and dressed, full of energy and sass and clear intentions for the winter. All day long we've been the ants in Aesop's fable, scurrying around the village to prepare it for winter. We may not love the work we do here, but we are proud of the work we've done today. We may not love the work, but we are accountable for it in ways we will never likely be again for the rest of our lives. At Holden, it is impossible to hide laziness or incompetence. Over the course of the next eight months, if something goes wrong, we will know whom to blame. And we will do so, sometimes openly, sometimes behind the closed door of a chalet, sometimes under our breath as we wake to a forty-degree room because someone has forgotten to stoke. The world of the village is small enough that there will be no escape from the truth of what we do and, by extension, who we are. In a few months, we will know each other too well.

But tonight, we know each other just enough. Enough that Miriam seems to contain a secret world of women and crowded streets and dim sum. Enough that the honey-grass scent of just-showered Lucas is unfamiliar and sweet, that his concentration as he rolls cigarette after cigarette seems artistic and precise. Enough that Finn's sudden headstand demonstration, Aaron's quiet retreat behind a pair of sunglasses, and Jeremy's whiskey-induced commentary feel like the first gestures of characters in a play, each movement still mysterious enough that anything could happen next.

We walk to dinner in a single file line down the brick path connecting Chalet Hill to the Ark and dining hall. The sky is deepening. We are divers sinking down from the surface of the sea, light dissolving, oxygen retreating, the new world we've chosen rising swiftly around us. I train my eyes on the outline of Aaron's bobbing bunny ears and follow the others into the night.

The next day, just after lunchtime, the letter from my Intended arrives. I read it in the dining hall cleaning closet. He says he is not coming to the village with my stereo and my snowshoes. He is going to Italy with another woman for three weeks instead. He tells me it makes him sick to write the words, that I must know how much he still loves me. He tells me he is doing what I wanted.

The closet has a swinging door with a quarter-sized hole where the handle used to be. The shelves contain jugs of vinegar. Gallon ice cream buckets filled with scrubbing powder. There are funnels with white cleaning residue on their spouts, a box of spray bottle heads, a box of mousetraps. The edges of the used green scrubbies curl like the red fortune teller fish I gave out as prizes at my fourth grade birthday party. Heat from our palms made the cellophane fish writhe, and the way a fish moved corresponded with a one-word summary of a "love style." Devoted. Passionate. Fickle. The fish lifted its head and tail or just its head. The fish raised its fins or flipped over entirely. But it wasn't the fortune we wanted. It was the way, for the first time, we saw the way the warmth from our bodies could cause another body to move. But now my Intended is gone, really gone, and the heat of my skin is useless from so far away.

Instead of returning to work, I retreat to my room. The ceiling slopes; the radiator clanks. Scott and Christine, the high school and elementary teacher respectively, live on the floor below me. When they brew beer or bake homemade crackers, my room fills with the scent. Today, when I cannot rid the tremors from my body or stop the sobs that heave through my chest, I ask my mother to tell Scott that I have fallen ill and will be unable to return to the school in the afternoon. I know he will recognize the lie. But I also know that my life has irrevocably changed. Work is the furthest thing from my mind.

Scrapbooking After Eden

Though there is some snowfall in October, the snow begins in earnest in November. Fat, wet flakes and light, dry ones. Flakes like pellets and flakes that turn into the wet sightlessness of rain. First the ground is warm and absorbs the snow; then the temperature drops and the snow accumulates. When the sun shines the snow is frosting, is glitter, is gorgeous accessory. When the clouds come the lightness disappears and the snow is weight, is the hair that overshadows the face, is a paralyzing force. What you feel about the snow, and the village beneath it, depends on knowledge, on whether you have loved the thing enough to see it for what it is.

Guests see the village as a life-sized snow globe, as Eden in winter. Many guests are from Minnesota so they know snow, but winter is different here. In Minnesota, the snow remains white only on roofs and in the middle of large fields. Everywhere else, it absorbs the detritus of the world: exhaust fumes, dog piss, Diet Coke, sorority vomit. Here in the village, the snow remains pure and virginal and unsullied. Guests spend their days, as they should, curled around novels and cups of cocoa in the dining hall or tromping through the forest in snowshoes from REI (bought specifically for this particular trip). And their vision of the village extends to the staff as well. We are salt of the earth people, a little ragged around the edges, a little unwashed and unshaved, but full of good cheer nonetheless. A reporter from a local travel magazine once wrote an article about the village in which he described the staff as "hearty." He described the minestrone soup and the fresh bread using the same term. It's not unnatural for visitors at a romantic locale to do this—if you visit a five-star resort in Jamaica, your poolside waiter becomes a part of your vision of the place. He's a prop, anonymous as a palm tree or water float.

We all want to know that Eden exists. We want to believe we've set foot inside it and that we might be able to go there again. Usually we think of Eden as a place, but now that he has vanished, I can't help thinking of my Intended in the same way. Part of the problem with longing is that you perpetually believe that the moment behind you is far superior to the one within which you are currently residing. There can be no happiness here, because it is all back there, glinting maniacally in the sun.

I have spread out, across the floor of my room, the contents of a huge box of photos from the relationship with my Intended. Three years worth of mountain vistas and cocktail dresses and holding hands in front of large bodies of water. If I put these photos in a scrapbook, if I make a narrative of the relationship, then I can weep a little, remember a little, and then put the scrapbook on a shelf and forget about it. The Indigo Girls are wailing about the land of Canaan on my stereo and I have a glue stick, rubber cement, markers, and scissors at the ready. My half-filled mug of wine is balanced precariously on my recently acquired copy of the *AWP Official Guide to Writing Programs*. In a few days I will be twenty-three years old.

It is summer. I am nineteen. My mother and I sit in the snack bar at Holden, hot fudge pooling around mint chocolate chip in our thick glass sundae dishes. Across the road we see a boy-man practicing tricks on a mountain bike. He is shirtless and deeply tanned, his back arched over the bike, the lines of his calves and biceps shifting almost imperceptibly as he turns the wheel to the right, to the left. His curly brown hair falls over his eyes, the whole mop shaking slightly as he eases the front tire over a stone step. He wears swimming trunks slung low enough that we can see the two bands of muscles that run, one from the right hip and one from the left, to his groin. I think of *National Geographic* specials in which whole teams of silver fish turn and dive, swoop and glisten, together as a single unit. There is that smoothness and grace to his body, a sheen that seems to contain multitudes. My mother and I eat our ice cream and watch the display appreciatively. "He must have the IQ of a geranium," she says.

He doesn't. His lips are dry but soften when I kiss them one week later. We miss Vespers.

I am astounded by his body and he is astounded by mine. Our bodies are beautiful. Our bodies are perpetually ripe, perpetually in a state of heavy dangling from a weary branch. We lay naked on the warm stones by Railroad Creek. We hike. We swing dance. He is this year's village plumber. He wears Carhartt pants and no shirt, whistles his way across the village with a huge wrench balanced over his shoulder. He tells me about his grandparents' farm: wild peacocks and apple trees. "Idyllic," he says. I tell him about being an unaccompanied minor by the age of four, about playing *Don't Break the Ice* in our family therapist's office. I place raspberries in the shape of a heart on his tanned, brown belly. I love the taste of his body, its salt and story so different from my own.

I fly back to Minnesota at the end of the summer and he remains at Holden. Our letters are like all love letters, generalized clichés about love peppered with mundane details. He installs a sprinkler system in the Holden garage and I write a paper about the Arpilleristas in Chile who sewed to resist the Pinochet regime. For my birthday he weaves a rug on one of the village looms and then transforms it into a backpack. He includes a copy of *The Giving Tree*, his favorite book. Inside is a peacock feather from his grandparents' farm. When I visit him he remembers how much cream to put in my coffee. We have sex for the first time in his childhood bed below a poster of a mountainous landscape with Hughes' "Dream Deferred" poem as the caption. I go to Ecuador for a semester abroad. I work with orphans and eat sweet rolls made with lard and listen to Ani Difranco on my walkman. He messes up his tailbone trying to snowboard over a jump on Chalet Hill, does garbology in the sleet and rain and snow, fills his Nalgene with yerba mate tea every morning and finishes it by noon.

I return to Holden the following June. We have sex on every surface imaginable: beds, couches, table tops, daisy fields, shaggy green carpet, etc., etc. We are certain our bodies are magical, that no one knows what we know. We carry the joy of this secret in our limbs, walk everywhere as though the Red Sea has parted just for us, as though we know the walls of water will hold. One hot August afternoon, when we can find no relief from the heat, we borrow bikes and pedal down the road to a place cleverly called Nine Mile since it is nine miles up the road from Lake Chelan. We park our bikes in bracken and scuff our way down to Railroad Creek. At Nine Mile the creek separates into two branches; the one nearer the road is ideal for swimming. We undress and walk out onto a fallen tree.

The water here moves so slowly it is barely perceptible. We track the movement in the pine needles swirling across the surface, in the aspen leaf that parades through the shadow the tree trunk casts. Fifty yards away, the other branch of the creek rushes forward, the speed and tumult of the water disguising what lies beneath. Over here, the sunlight illuminates the space below the surface: brown and cloudy but spangled by specks of sediment turned golden. It is the room in childhood where time stilled and the motes of dust provided the only sense of motion. We slip into that brown room, my Intended and me. The cold of the water is clamor and clash. We pull ourselves from the stream, our bodies turned to tin, and make love on the bank until we are malleable again.

Memory is like this. The past, what really happened, rushes by. That version is unchanging but so swift we can barely see what lies beneath. Memory is the diverted, slower stream, the one that feigns transparency. The one that we can slip into and crawl out of with someone we loved. Love. There is what happened and the story we tell ourselves about what happened. And somewhere in between is the truth. We want Eden still. But given access, our knowledge doesn't permit us to live there happily. We are outside of happiness, longing to be allowed back in.

My late night scrapbooking session, coupled with the wine and tears that came with it, makes Monday morning come too soon. From the window in the dining hall, I watch blue fog smooth across the hips of Buckskin mountain. I'm sipping coffee and dunking craisins into the mottled wet slum of my cold oatmeal. Across the road, the snow on the roof of the village Center is the height of my forearm. Over at the silver counter, Lucas is chopping carrots, the movements of his knife rhythmic and precise. When he pauses to shift his glasses up the bridge of his nose he catches me watching him, smiles and winks, then returns to the carrots, the flicking of silver quickening slightly.

My journal is open; I'm a fan of the unconscious, of automatic writing and so I make myself scribble uncontrollably for half an hour before work every morning. Today I've written a riff that began with the prompt "I can't get out of bed this morning because . . ." and ended with an image of green worms inhabiting the face of my Intended. I want to be a writer, but no matter where I begin I always seem to end in the same place: grief. Yesterday, the Intended and I were frozen figures in Pompeii. The day before that, I wrote a villanelle that included the repeated lines "black widow spiders masticate their mates" and "the chosen male is always willing bait."

"You made short work of those craisins," says Aaron, prompting me out of my feigned writerly reverie. Then Aaron's gaze drifts from the bowl of cereal to my face and hair. The supply of hot water in my chalet is unpredictable and showering generally leaves me goose bumped and wondering about the extra layer of fat that has attached itself to my belly. So usually I don't shower in the morning. I tie my long blond hair back and put on my glasses and cover my body with a turtleneck and sweatshirt and vest. Today, I actually managed to shower and to dress myself in a semi-attractive green sweater. My hair is mostly dry since I've been sitting at the table for half an hour and I've taken off my glasses so that the vista of blue fog crossing the mountains will look even more blurry and nostalgic than it already is.

Aaron hands me a fresh cup of coffee. "You know, Kaethe, when you take the time to wash and brush your hair, you're actually kind of attractive."

I roll my eyes. "Why thank you, Aaron. I believe you just made my day."

"You should come skiing with me after work."

"You know I'm not coordinated enough to ski."

"That's true," says Aaron. He takes a sip of coffee, admires the view, and then says consolingly, "At least your hair looks nice."

"Maybe," I say, "but I'm sure it won't by lunchtime."

"Oh Kaethe," says Aaron, "I would never have expected it to."

I know going for a ski with Aaron would be healthy for me in the same way I know my relationship with Aaron is good for me. Aaron is short. A brown beard and boxy chest. Aaron is both a true friend and a terrific flirt. He has the amazing ability to both listen carefully to the excruciatingly boring details of my woe while simultaneously reminding me that he wouldn't mind getting in my pants. When we talk about his depression, we treat it like dishteam or garbology, like it's a mildly crappy necessity, like it will pass. Every day after work, Aaron heads off to ski in a suit that looks like it was made for an automotive attendant. Down the road between fifteen-foot banks of snow he goes in the dimming gray light. He doesn't worry about the cougars, the darkness, the cold. This world is not so different from the next. The seam is thin. Some days the impossibility of living in either place overwhelms him.

There was more snow last night, six puffy inches, and as I walk the half block to the school after breakfast I leave behind a perfect set of prints. Singular and lonely. I think about the anecdote about Jesus and the footprints and the beach. I think about how much I hate that anecdote. In case you haven't had the pleasure, the story goes that a man dreams his life as a walk along the beach. Most of the time, there are two sets of footprints, one set belongs to him and one set belongs to Jesus. The man is overjoyed to learn about his constant Christian companion until he realizes that at the times he suffered the most, there is only one set of footprints. He reads this as abandonment. *No*, says Jesus, *those were the times I carried you*. Cue tears. The thing that bugs me about this is that it takes Jesus saying *I was present, I was with you*, for the man to feel that this is true. Of course I want God there in the midst of my suffering, but I want to feel God's presence, want to know with certainty that I haven't been abandoned.

Two nights after I received the letter from my Intended, I snuck down to the village Center in the middle of the night. The village Center is actually a large gymnasium and was used as such during the mining days. We still use if for the occasional game of soccer or basketball in the winter, but mostly it's used during the summer as the main worship space. In 1976, Richard Caemmerer painted the ceiling. This result is not a Sistine Chapel look-alike. There are no typical biblical images, no lions cozied to lambs, no angels with hearkening smiles, no fisherman casting their nets into turbulent seas; instead, the ceiling looks like a liturgical acid trip. Bold swaths of color swirl and divide and sometimes manifest into recognizable images: a trout, a star, a snowflake, an egg. Though I have been staring at that ceiling every summer for twenty-two years, I can barely describe it. I could never sketch it. It's shifty and mysterious and jubilant and disturbing. Just below the west side of the ceiling, above the stage (used for mediocre theatrical events for over eighty years) large oak letters spell out: "God Gives Seasons for Gladness of Heart."

In the summer the village Center (or VC) fills up with bodies and singing and clapping and breath. The entire village, regardless of actual religious belief, shows up for Vespers every night. Vespers is one of the monastic hours, the one that comes at evening time, when day is turning to dusk. Sometimes other monastic services are held, like Matins (morning) or Compline (night), but Vespers is the only service celebrated daily. And attending Vespers is a requirement of the Holden community. You show up, whether God is your thing or not, because it matters to have everyone present and together for a portion of each day. It matters not because everyone needs to rehearse a particular dogma together, but because when you live this closely to so many others, it is important to be present with them, to be quiet with them, for a few minutes every day. We are together at mealtimes too, but mealtimes also include conversation, and conversation can be muddled with anger or cloaked with desire, depending on whether you are sitting with the person who forgot to stoke or the one who caressed you in the jacuzzi. Vespers is about unison, perhaps a feigned or artificial unison, but unison nonetheless. We stand together and sit together, we sing together and speak words together and when a child remarks, "Mama, church is boring" during a moment of quiet prayer, we swing our heads in unison toward the sound and chuckle for the appropriate length of time.

It is right to be suspicious of this kind of unison. It is right to squint one's eyes and think vaguely about soldiers marching in uniform lines under Hitler's watchful eye. Unison of any sort requires a giving up of the self, at least for a brief moment in time, and of course it matters to what or whom one is giving oneself. The white, educated middle class in America has become very good at this kind of suspicion. Our knee-jerk reaction to organized religion is to mention cults and Kool-Aid and lemmings, to feel satisfied about our own intellectual superiority, and to write "those people" off as stupid. I have thought all those things. I like to talk about religion but the truth is that the actual practice of faith, the swelling of it in my heart, it doesn't come easily to me. I forget to pray and when I do I get distracted. In college I took a class on feminist theology but refused to go to daily chapel because they didn't use inclusive language for God. It was easier to remain cynical of the church, to be smoking cigarettes in the shadows outside it, then to be inside and implicated.

To practice a religion is, in some ways, to take responsibility for it. This is why it's easier to be spiritual than religious. You can pick and choose the things that make sense and feel right. You don't have to deal with the idiots who still think God is a man, who still think marriage is just about men and women, who want to preach the tomb without resurrection, damnation instead of grace. Yes, following anything or anyone (be that ideal religious, political, aesthetic, or romantic) without thought is silly and potentially disastrous. But so is hanging onto the intellect at the expense of participating in something that moves us beyond the borders of ourselves, that makes us vulnerable in ways that suspicion and cynicism do not allow.

So although sometimes I find Vespers to be boring or pretentious or aesthetically suspect, I go every evening so that for twenty or thirty minutes of the day I can practice moving beyond myself. I go because I have made a promise to this community to attend. And I go because I love the space where we worship. The VC, with its acid trip ceiling and altar standing just to the left of the free throw line, is the most real church I know.

That's why, two nights after my Intended left, I snuck into the village Center. I wanted to pray. But it was October and the VC was unheated. The lights take a significant amount of energy to run, so, rather than risk causing a power outage that would plunge the entire village into darkness, I did without. In the resolute dimness, all I felt were the drafts coming in the door and the numbness sinking into my fingertips. I couldn't even will myself to cry, which was strange since I seem to be able to cry at the drop of a hat anywhere else in the village. I prayed but I felt no kind of assurance, no mystic calm settling into my heart, no deep sense of being loved beyond all measure. I just felt cold. If I was being carried by Jesus than he had drugged me up pretty good. When I left the VC, there was no black swath of sky with meaningful scattering of stars; the clouds were close and low, like God wanted me housed in a poorly lit basement office space.

Today is similarly cloudy and although my hair looks nice, thinking of the emptiness of that night makes me scuff my footprints in the snow; the pattern I leave now looks like it was made by a drunk derelict, by someone anonymous and unrecognizable.

I remove my boots when I enter the school and put on my slippers. We all wear slippers once it begins to snow to keep the wet and dirt from being tracked from room to room. I take off my coat and hat and enter the elementary room. Christine, the elementary school teacher, hands me a stack of papers to photocopy. The hallways and supply closet are unheated so I put my coat and hat back on and spend the next hour in the supply closet, watching the green bar of light slide back and forth beneath my palms. I study the extra boxes of markers, of ball point pens, of glue sticks. Post-it notes, index cards, construction paper. Back and forth goes the bar. Out slide the sheets. *Color seven beans green. Color two beans purple. Circle three stars. Put a square around one star.* Scissors, masking tape, scotch tape, duct tape. Mousetraps, paper towels, glue. *Draw three fish in the ocean. Draw two birds in the nest.* The closet fills with the scent of photocopies, an acidy warmth that settles inside the nostrils. The green light is a search light.

The green light is a beacon that guides the airplanes in. The green light is comforting the copier, is stroking its belly. When the last paper has rolled through and settled with its peers, I close my eyes and bring the entire warm stack to my cheek. Behind my closed lids the green light moves back and forth. I am dizzy but I stand there until the papers grow cold.

Photocopying complete, I take Forrest and Tasha, ages four and five respectively, into the library. Two ant farms sit on a low wooden bench against one wall. About a week ago we planted beans in the ant farms. Every day Tasha and Forrest dutifully record the growth. They are still young enough that any kind of intense studiousness looks darling. Tasha's hair falls across her face. She presses so hard with the pencil that the fibers of the wooden bench show up like a secret rubbing below the image of roots she is trying to render. Forrest is both younger and less patient. Though he initially tries to mimic the spread of the shoots from the beans, he quickly grows bored and lets the shoots wonder willy-nilly all over the paper until it looks like if one parted the lines, Sleeping Beauty might be there, eyes closed, sweet breath slipping out between ruby lips.

"Done," says Forrest.

"Almost done," says Tasha.

Forrest experiments with hopping on one foot. Then he lies on his back on one of the tumbling mats in the center of the room and raises his legs. "I'm touching the ceiling with my toes," he says.

"No you're not," says Tasha without looking. She adds a tiny curlicue to her rendition of the final bean's growth and then lays down beside Forrest and raises her legs.

"Mine are touching more than yours."

"Let's pretend to be animals," I say. As I have been instructed to say. This is PE. We spend the next fifteen minutes parading up and down the two blue mats. First we are dogs. Then cats. We are recognizable as frogs, elephants, horses. Then I let them choose and our gestures grow less transparent. We are vultures. We are cougars. We are dinosaurs. We are injured sharks. We are camels with sore throats. We are fawns with a hundred invisible spots. No one walking by the room right now would be able to tell us what we are.

I am twenty. After the summer my Intended moves to Minnesota and enrolls at the college I attend. We live in the basement of an old woman's house. We hang tie-dyed sheets on the wall and make bookcases out of old lumber and cinder blocks. For my birthday he sews me a tank top that ties in three places across my back. I am co-leader of the student justice organization on campus. We go to meetings together with the flush of sex still high in our cheeks. First his mother says to be careful of me. My parents are divorced so I am damaged goods. Then his father has an affair and his parents divorce and he puts his head in my lap and we are damaged goods together. He teaches me to love butter and chardonnay, encourages me not to shave my legs. Two years into the relationship my heart still jumps every time he enters a room.

I graduate. We move to Berkeley. We live in a beautiful house with four other Holden friends. Across the street is the Mattress Mart and down the block is the Indian restaurant with cloth flowers on the tables. The flowers even have fake drops of dew glistening on the petals. I teach Spanish in the Oakland Hills. He takes the BART to San Francisco State where he takes classes in urban geography and landscape ecology. On the weekends we get high and smuggle pear cider into the movie theater and watch in stupefied silence films about animated ogres or the insect life of a meadow. I am in love with how much I love him. I am in love with how much he loves me. I am in love with what the windows reflect, our bodies holding hands.

Then one day, walking down a hill in San Francisco, streetcar tracks to our left, Bay spread out at our feet, I say, lightly, that I plan to keep my last name when we get married. He looks at me, concerned and puzzled. He shakes his head a little, as though trying to rid his hair of dandruff or the fragments of leaves. Then he smiles. "Okay," he says. "I'll take your name. That would be fine."

"No," I say. "I want to keep my own name."

"Then we'll hyphenate," he says.

"No," I say. "I want my name."

And that is the end.

This is not true, of course. The past rushes by, carrying all of our reasons for ending: the fights and the coldness, the pot and the boredom and my own inability to commit. But this is the moment that slows for me, that I slip into and out of when I need to understand.

At 3:00 the students leave the school for the day. My contract stipulates that I need to work until 4:00 so Scott, the high school teacher, has devised interminable and unnecessary tasks for me to complete if there isn't grading or clean-up to do. The worst task is double-checking the library catalog against the actual books we have on the shelves. To make the task bearable, I bring my small gray stereo and a cooling cup of coffee to the library with me. I play a Rebecca Riots song on repeat that includes a line about faith and change and learning useful lessons while dwelling in a hellhole. I cry a little. I halfheartedly spray the tumbling mats with a cleaning solution and run a rag over the places where Forrest and Tasha and I marched a few hours earlier. Outside the window, the playground equipment is up to its knees in snow. The bottom of the slide is covered and the post and beam arch, swing removed, now looks like a gallows in waiting. The current library catalog is printed on old computer paper, the kind with a row of detachable holes on either side. When I grow tired of running my finger along laminated spines, weary of checking whether we have four copies of *The Bean Trees* or five, I occupy myself with removing the margins of the pages along those faint, detachable lines.

At 3:55 I walk over to the bench where the beans are dutifully sprouting in the ant farms. I study the shoots, bone-white and slightly pointed at the tips. Their route to the sky is indirect but persistent nonetheless. Though of course I can't see them moving there is a sense of mobility in their reach. I loosen the knobs on the sides of the first ant farm and swing the entire body of the farm in a 180-degree turn. Now the shoots are pointing down instead of up. We will spend the next week watching their ability to determine the difference between heaven and earth, recording carefully their ability to right themselves.

After work I trudge up to Chalet Six, my parents' chalet, to borrow my mother's rubber cement; my own supply was depleted in the scrapbooking frenzy last night. As I walk up the hill I have to step to the side a few times as both guest and village kids come careening down on toboggans and inner tubes. The elementary girls have fashioned a small jump (more like a bump) in front of Chalet Six. As I turn up my parents' walkway I hear the sound of a jaw snapping shut as a particularly brave sledder takes the jump head on. When I walk into the chalet the temperature seems to be approximately the same as outside. "Did someone forget to stoke?" I call cheerily. Peter and my sixteen-year-old brother, Michael, are standing in the dining room in front of two broken windows. They thought a bird was responsible for the damage, or maybe a lone football, but it turns out it was the ice. The icicles that line the eaves of the chalet roofs grow long. When the temperatures warm, the entire mass of snow on the roof inches down slightly, icicles included. But instead of moving downward vertically, these icicles turned inward toward the house.

My mother, who can't resist a cleaning job, is already on her hands and knees on the floor. Her fingertips are bloody. She can't tell the glass from the ice.

I steal both rubber cement and a day-old brownie and trudge back to my own chalet. From the porch I see Aaron setting off on his skis, the gray of his suit retreating into the encroaching dusk. I am convinced that I can finish the scrapbook project by dinnertime, though by this point I am also equally convinced of the futility of the project as a method for surmounting grief.

The last picture I have of the Intended was taken on September 2nd, the first day of school. This was just over two months ago, before he left the village for good, before I began hoping for his return. The first day of school at Holden is an exercise in ridiculousness. No one lives farther than a block from the school, but on the first day one of the yellow school buses is driven (by a costumed buck-toothed driver holding a can of beer) up Chalet Hill. The bus stops at each chalet, and sometimes in between, picking up the students and other lone villagers as it goes. Parents make a huge deal out of their children leaving. Mothers emerge in bathrobes, faces covered in cucumber masks and hair done up in rollers. Fathers smoke pipes and read newspapers on the porches of the chalets. A few of the mothers hang laundry across the road and rush around hanging it up and taking it down as the school bus progresses.

In addition to the parental farewells, the rest of the village gets into the act, often in ways that are entirely nonsensical. Kent brings a TV and recliner out onto the side of the road and pretends to watch it as the bus rolls by. The residents of Chalet Thirteen don hula apparel and bone necklaces and stir up the bus's exhaust fumes with a solemn, bare-bellied dance. Heather, crafts coordinator extraordinaire and clad in neon orange, pretends to be a crossing guard; my brother inexplicably wears a jester's hat. Two of the tallest men in the village dress in skirts and blond braided wigs and carry lunchboxes the size of suitcases that say "Heidi" and "Helga." When the bus completes the loop of Chalet Hill and is within a hundred yards of the school, Jeremy and Aaron and my Intended hijack the bus. They call themselves the Plumber Liberation Army and they divert the bus all the way up to the tailings and back, the kids laughing uproariously in the back. Within ten minutes they are back, and the Plumber Liberation Army members usher the kids off the bus, holding the hands of the little ones, winking at the high schoolers.

But this means that in the last picture I possess of my Intended I cannot see his face. He is standing on the grass in front of Chalet Two, holding a fake gun make of PVC pipe. He wears navy long underwear with the letters PLA stuck to the front of the shirt in masking tape. A black facemask covers his head, which is turned to the right, watching for the approach of the bus. Because the long johns are a size too large, the fabric hangs loosely. Even his body is unrecognizable to me now.

But then I laughed as I watched them hijack the bus because it was September 2nd, 2001, and terrorism was a word that existed far from home, on the other side of Eden, a garden from which we had not yet been expelled.

DECEMBER

Coming to Consensus

"I don't see what the problem is," says Aaron, "if 'Jingle Bells' helps them wake up in the morning, let them play it. What difference does it make?"

The community members in the Fireside room are steadily growing either more irate or more comatose. It's nearing 9 p.m. on a Wednesday night and we are gathered for our weekly community meeting. The Fireside Room is, true to its name, actually arranged around a fire pit in the center of the room. The pit is constructed out of stones, cemented together into a two-foot-high circle that contains a shallow bed of sand. Into the sand we place religious or semi-religious decorative icons. Sometimes a cross made out of driftwood, sometimes a few cairns of river stones, sometimes a collection of vases with impossibly delicate necks, spun by our own village potter. At the moment an advent wreath occupies the center space. Since we hold Vespers in the Fireside Room just before the community meeting on Wednesdays, one of Advent candles is still dripping waxy red tears. Wooden captain's chairs circle the fire pit, and most of the community is settled into these with the people closest to the fire pit propping their Mukluk or Sorel-clad feet on the stones.

I am sitting in the balcony of the Fireside Room, my chin resting on one of the smooth blond beams of the railing and my feet dangling over the head of Kent, who sits directly below me. Kent, like many other villagers, has taken up knitting and from time to time he brings the truncated scarf close to his face to count stitches. Behind me, Lucas leans against the wall, taking sips from his wine-filled Nalgene bottle. To my left, Jeremy stretches prone on his back, green felt hat covering his face.

We've already shared Joys, Frustrations, and Concerns ("I am thankful to Mark for taking my dishteam on Friday," "I am frustrated by the constant mess in the dining hall living room space," "I am concerned about those I saw skiing into an avalanche-danger area yesterday"), we've scooted through announcements relatively quickly, and we are now onto the potentially longest portion of the meeting: Issue to be Resolved by Consensus. Today's issue is whether the cooks should be permitted to play Christmas carols in the kitchen during Advent.

"For me, to do so is ignoring the posture of Advent," says Christy, who plans to go to seminary next year. "For me, Advent is about waiting, about patience and expectation. If we're trying to reside in this kind of emotional space, then it seems important to withhold from ourselves the joyful elements of Christmas until Christ himself arrives in our midst."

There is nodding. I look at Lucas and roll my eyes.

He raises his Nalgene. "To baby Jesus," he whispers, handing the bottle to me.

"To Santa," I reply. The taste of the boxed Franzia feels like both punishment and reward.

In 1978 a man named John Howard Yoder, a theologian and Mennonite, came to the village as a member of the summer teaching staff. He stood at the front of the Fireside Room, bearded and bespectacled, sweat stains growing on his short-sleeved dress shirt, and contended that most Christians preferred not to think of Jesus as political. They wanted their politics in one place and their religion in another. Religion was an internal process and politics an external predicament. There was lots of nodding, lots of "uh-huhing" from the Holden audience. "For instance," said Yoder, "some people like their politics in a city and their religion in a rural mountain village." The uh-huhing stopped.

Yoder went on: Martin Luther was certainly a fan of this division; in his estimation, there were two kingdoms, one run by God and the other by humans. Luther's desire to understand things this way came as a response to the Catholic idea of the world governed entirely by the church—and Luther didn't much care for the results of that ideology. But this idea of the two kingdoms, of a separation of religion and politics, was not, in Yoder's estimation, working out so well.

Jesus, he explained in his slow halting voice, was very political. Jesus wanted us to give away our wealth and befriend our enemies; you can't get more political than that. And, Yoder claimed, if you're busy thinking that Jesus wasn't political, it's likely that you just don't feel comfortable following his politics.

Yoder wasn't just interested in the theology. He was interested in the practice of theology. First and foremost, he told the Holden community that summer, if you wanted the hills made low and the valleys made high, if you wanted everything evened out, you needed to make sure everyone's voice was heard. If there was a communal decision to be made, you couldn't just cast ballots or nod obediently while the dictator spoke. Everyone should have the chance to speak and everyone should learn to listen: "Consensus arises uncoerced out of open conversation. There is no voting in which a majority overruns a minority and no decision of a leader by virtue of his office. The only structure this process needs is the moderating that keeps it orderly and the recording of the conclusions reached."

The Quakers knew how to do this. So did the Mennonites. And in the late 1970s, the decision to begin listening to oppressed voices was a choice made actively outside of the church too.

And so Holden Village took up the practice of consensus decision-making, with varying degrees of success.

It's 1979. I'm six months old. My mother and father are having dinner at the house of Steve and Gick and no one has mentioned that the chicken is bloody near the bone. No one has mentioned the chicken, but my father has proclaimed the buttered carrots to be *unbelievably delicious* and my mother has said, *Can I get the recipe for this salad dressing, is it rosemary, is that what I taste?* Everyone is still scooting the chicken around on their plates when the phone rings. Steve sighs. On the other end he knows is a man named Walt whom he is going to disappoint. He is going to say to Walt, *I know I promised to come in August but I cannot come to your remote mountain retreat center in August.* Gick clears the dishes while Steve talks. My mother scrapes the chicken bones into the trash, trying to think of what word she would use to describe the color of the chicken at its most raw. My father, left alone at the dining room table, is fiddling with the centerpiece Gick proudly refers to as a Zen garden. It is a box of sand with rocks and bits of vegetation. *Using this rake*, Gick explained before dinner, *you comb the sand. It helps you think less.* My father is writing *shit* in careful script in the sand. If he's careful enough, if Steve and Gick don't notice, he can tell my mother as they lie in bed together that night, their heads at the foot of the bed and the breeze from the window lapping across their cheeks, their necks, their clavicles.

Suddenly Steve is in the doorway, his hand muffling the phone receiver, saying, *Do you want to do it, Mark? Teach, I mean. Sounds like a good deal. Mountains in August.* My father, pleased Steve hasn't noticed the sand or the tiny rake between his fingers, says, *Sure, I think so, why not? Ricki, what do you think?* My mother, holding an oily plate, shrugs. *Sure,* she says. *Why not?* My father brushes the sand off his palms. *Rose,* thinks my mother, *scarlet, salmon, begonia, blush.*

We fly from Chicago to Seattle. On the plane my mother drinks Tab and feeds me bits of ice that she crushes first between her teeth. My father holds me up to the window and says *mountain, snow, peak.* I pat the plexiglass. We take a bus from Seattle to Wenatchee. The mountains are tall and dark and green, a maze our bus crawls through. We drive farther and the mountains shrink, turn brown and brittle. The Columbia River is a whip of blue. The orchards are military rows of green. We spend the night at a hotel swollen with the scent of smoke and decorated with paintings of boats balanced precariously on thunderhead seas. In the morning a ferry takes us up Lake Chelan and deposits us at a landing where two school buses wait. I touch my forehead to the glass of the bus and my mother wipes the dust off my nose. I try to stand on my father's thighs but the muscles there shift back and forth over his bones. We climb up nine switchbacks, the lake turning to a puddle below us. We pass a dwindling waterfall, alumroot and chicory, lodgepole pine and fir. Then, on the left side of the road, there is orange behind the scrim of trees, orange so bright it must be manufactured, orange like Kraft cheese powder piled 150 feet into the air. The piles of orange are tailings, the detritus produced in the process of separating mineral from rock, the process of separating what is of worth from what matters least. Then, abruptly, the bus jerks to a halt and we are there.

I don't remember the visit but the photos from that time show a chubby, happy, blonde baby. I am crawling in green overalls down a cobblestone path, I am standing naked, proudly holding onto a white radiator for balance, I am mastering a wooden rocking horse with the help of a woman with a Farrah Fawcett haircut. In one photo, I am riding in a backpack on my father's shoulders, the two of us posed on the flat top of one of the tailings piles. Behind us, a row of firs, and mountains slanting diagonally into the sky.

That summer, my parents didn't attend any meetings that featured consensus decision-making (most of those occurred during the winter months), but my father did lead forums around questions like "Was Hiroshima Necessary?" and "Can There Be Such a Thing as a Christian Soldier?"

The photographs from the following summer feature mountains shrouded in mist, three rainbow trout laid out beside a fishing net, my father squatting with me before a garden filled with wild irises. There are families and couples I don't remember, dressed in the wide-legged jeans and tight-fitting poly-cotton blend t-shirts of the time. There is my father, the village philosopher, dressed in a blue velvet robe and matching velvet mortarboard, hammering a set of faux theses to a tree. There are children lined up before a puppet stage, their hands wearing the puppet costumes like gloves, the Styrofoam heads of the puppets riding on their index fingers. My mother, the puppetry teacher, stands proudly beside them.

Now it seems important that there is only one photo of my mother and father and I together. The picture was taken on the day of the village Renaissance festival. My father wears a loose salmon-colored shirt, belted at the waist, with decorative laces between the breastbone and neck. My mother wears a gallon ice cream container, covered with tinfoil, on her head. The small hole cut in the front of the bucket reveals her eyes and the top half of her nose. She carries a garbage can lid as a shield. My father has his arm around my mother's shoulders and my mother holds me: white-blonde pigtails, cloth napkin tucked into my shirt neck, eyes squinting unhappily into the sun. That is the last picture I possess of the three of us together. The next summer, as my mother set out folded outfits, sunscreen, bug repellent, and snacks for the trip to Holden, my father approached her with the plane tickets in his hand. *I'm not going*, he said. But what my mother heard was: *I am asking you to leave me.*

It's now 9:30pm. Two community members have cried and one has used profanity. Jeremy is snoring gently. Lucas has finished the wine and is now tipping the bottle upside down and then right side up to watch the last dregs finger their way up and down the sides of BPA-free plastic.

"I just feel like we're smart enough as human beings to do both things at once," says Heather, an inkle loom perched between her knees. "I mean,

I think I can hear 'Oh Come All Ye Faithful' and still retain the posture of Advent. It's not rocket science." She breaks a purple thread with her teeth.

Although I think this particular issue is ridiculous, many of the issues we devote time to discussing are not. From the time of its inception as a Lutheran retreat center, the village has fostered continued debate around issues of theological, ethical, and social import. Should the village serve strictly vegetarian food? Should hunters be allowed to store guns in the village? Should the village purchase a satellite phone? Should the village be open to calling a gay or lesbian pastor? Although many of these questions deal specifically with an issue in the village, they point to a political world outside of it.

For instance, we spent much of September and October discussing how to respond as a community to the events of 9/11. Eventually, we agreed to write a letter and send it to local and national publications. My stepfather, Peter, and my friend Jamie and I drafted the letter together. In it, we explained that our community was grieving for the loss of so many lives, grieving for firefighters caught in the blaze and the passengers who fell terrified from the sky, for those who collapsed with the towers and the families who are still sorting through wreckage. We grieve, said the letter, but we are also suspicious of using words like "revenge" and "retaliation" and "justice" without words like "forgiveness" and "reflection" and "grace." We don't believe we should join hands with terrorists and sing "Kumbaya," but we are wary of using violence to respond to violence. We are concerned about who we become when we do so.

Jamie and Peter and I were proud of the letter and we displayed it using a yellowed overhead projector during a community meeting in early October. The projector fan whirred. The dim lights still managed to catch the sheen of silver on the duct tape used to repair loose patches of the thin crimson carpet. Everyone seemed to agree that we should send the letter, that this was our one voice singing out to the world. Everyone except Kent. Kent sat next to the fire ring, kitchen clogs on the stones, balanced on the back two legs of his captain's chair. All of his attention was focused on the hat he held in his hands, his first knitting accomplishment, now beginning to unravel along the brim. Kent is a big man, tall and long-limbed, and he usually stretches his body long, legs crossed at the ankles, arms thrown out over the backs of chairs beside him. But that day he was hunched over his knees and all I could see of his face, from my vantage point, was his dark brown hair flopping over his forehead and his eyebrows, drawn together like a descent of frozen swallows.

Everyone could see the resistance in Kent, not just me. When you live with sixty-five people in close proximity, you understand how their bodies work and move. You know where each person carries tension, how she sits, whether she leads with her chin or her chest when she walks. Sometimes sitting on the porch of our chalet, Jeremy guesses the identity of villagers walking toward us down the road long before their faces become recognizable.

"Do you want to say something, Kent?" asked Dave, the staff coordinator and meeting facilitator.

Kent shook his head and began to pull at the errant stitch on the hat.

"Does it seem like we have consensus?" asked Dave.

"Actually, Dave, I think it's pretty clear Kent isn't much of a fan of this idea," said Jeremy from the balcony, "though it's unclear to me what's going on with him right now or why he's not in favor of this letter, which seems pretty innocuous to me."

Kent had managed to squeeze most of the hat into his left fist. He was poking the rest of the material in with his right index finger.

"I agree with Jeremy," said Miriam. "Kent? We'd really like to hear what you have to say."

The silence in the room went on for a long time. The projector fan whirred. Knitting needles clicked and then stopped clicking. A section of snow slid down the roof and landed with a soft thump outside the windows. Someone cleared her throat. Someone sneezed. The fan whirred on.

Then Kent stood up abruptly, knocking his chair backward. He left the room, both fists clenched, the hat buried somewhere inside one. He didn't return.

The summer of 1981 my father was, of course, absent from all of the Holden photos. There is only one photo of my mother. She holds me but my face is not visible, only the curling blonde hair of one of my pigtails and an Oreo clutched in my left hand. The photo is black and white, my mother's hair pulled back from her face with a single barrette. She is smiling in the photo but the lower rims of her eyelids are puffy. She is smiling but for the first time I can see the starburst lines at the corners of her eyes.

In 1983 my mother moved to Minnesota and at the age of four I became an unaccompanied minor, flying alone once a month between my two houses. Oddly, I felt content during those flights, equally divided between my two lives, counting the flashes of light at the end of the wingtip. I'd read *James and the Giant Peach* and knew about the men who played in the clouds and I watched for them diligently. By 1984, both my parents had remarried; by 1985 both my stepmother and stepfather had been ushered into the Holden experience. I acquired step-siblings and half-siblings and an adopted sibling and my new brothers and sisters rotated through the village too. Every few years, the visits of my households overlapped and my family became the happy end of an after school special, the divorced family who vacations together in the utopian mountain village.

"Maybe there's some kind of compromise that could be reached?" suggests my mother tentatively, "like maybe the cooks play Christmas carols only in the early morning hours before other people are awake but then switch to other music after 7:30 or something?" A few villagers nod. One shrugs. One sighs. One moves her wool sweater up her arm to look coyly at her watch. It's 9:45.

One of the first directors of the village, Carroll Hinderlie, declared that the gospel lives through controversy. I think what he meant by this is that the work of Jesus, the political work, rarely gets done from a place of complicity or active passivity. I think he meant that the gospel is mysterious and contentious and if we get to a place where we think we understand it, we are likely to be in trouble. I think he meant that sometimes truth is found in the space where two ideas create enough friction against each other to make a kind of fire. The kind of fire that, as we understand it here in the wilderness, is necessary for new growth.

After my parents divorced and remarried, after I acquired step-siblings and half-siblings and an adopted sibling, my life swung back and forth between two distinct worlds.

My mother lived in Minnesota and my father in Indiana. My father jogged around the ponds of suburban developments and my mother ran marathons. My father and stepmother went to a Lutheran church with pea green pew cushions and a pastor who invited us over for pot roast with carrots and pearl onions. Peter, my stepfather, drove us in a maroon Volvo to a Catholic church where everyone worshiped in an auditorium and the lyrics of songs were projected onto a screen above a band that plucked out the tunes. My stepmother, Dorothy, kept her refrigerator stocked with half and half and olives and homemade jams and ranch dressing and bottles of tonic water. My mother kept hers stocked with soy milk and canola oil mayonnaise and organic blueberries and Kefir. Dorothy bought Jif and my mother bought peanut butter with the oil on top. Dorothy drank Tropicana and my mother slid cylinders of frozen juice out of the cardboard cans and mixed them into water with a wooden spoon. My mother and Peter took us to Mexico, to Haiti, to Guatemala, and the Dominican Republic. We stayed in hostels, in boarding houses, in hotels with bug-infested sheets. My father and Dorothy took us to South Carolina, to Florida, to resorts with tennis courts and beaches that reached right up to the windows of our lodgings. Dorothy lit a candle on the occasion of my twin brother and sister's baptism and kept a picture of each of us, framed and dusted, on top of the piano. My mother remembered my baptism only occasionally. She kept a photo of my two stepbrothers at one end of her dresser and a photo of Michael and me at the other end. From time to time my mother drank a glass of cheap red wine. My father drank two martinis every night.

Laundry chutes carried our dirty clothes to the basement at my father's house. Then a woman named Maria or Gloria or Inez would wash and fold and place the piles of clothing on the smooth mahogany of our dresser tops. In Minnesota, a white wicker hamper sat in the upstairs bathroom and my mother came, every day, and dug the clothes out by the armful. Peter was a well-known criminal defense attorney but my mom shopped mostly at Target, mostly wore turtlenecks and sweatshirts in the winter and old marathon t-shirts in the summer. My stepmother wrote books about practical theology and wore delicate dangling silver earrings and pretty tailored jackets and scarves. At bedtime, my mother left the hall light on and my door open a crack. My stepmother knelt with my brother and sister to say prayers. She sang to them "My Bonnie Lies Over the Ocean" and kissed them good night.

I watched and listened. If I was careful, I could fit seamlessly into both homes. But I noticed, over time, that life always went on in both households whether I was present or not. Although I was a welcome member of both homes, I was not a necessary part of either's design.

Then I graduated from college and moved to California with my Intended and I had to make choice after choice: fresh orange juice or frozen, wine or martini, Target or the new boutique, Jif or the peanut butter that took five minutes to stir. They weren't just choices; they were a formulation of loyalties. And most of the time, I couldn't bring myself to decide.

We decide, finally, that the cooks can play Christmas music during Advent as long as the music has no words. Instrumental collections featuring harps and hand bells are suggested.

"Fuck that," mumbles Lucas under his breath when consensus is finally established.

"Amen," offers Jeremy from under his hat.

"My room? More wine?" asks Lucas, his voice including both of us but his eyes focused on me. "I'm a two shift tomorrow so I can sleep in."

"I have to introduce kindergarteners to the planets at 8:30. Rain check?" I say.

"I'm in," says Jeremy, "but only if we can play Christmas carols while we drink."

"Done," says Lucas.

As we trail out of Koinonia, Jeremy and Lucas turn left toward Lodge Six; I head up the dining hall steps and onto the saw-dusted trail back to Chalet One, humming "Away in a Manger" under my breath.

Though 1980 was more or less the official end of my parents' relationship, in my mind the relationship actually ends two years earlier, before either of them had ever heard of Holden Village.

It is April 14, 1978. My parents are in New York, staying at a Sheraton seven blocks from Central Park. They have been living in dingy apartments for the last nine years, on couches and chairs covered and recovered in fabric to hide the stains and the worn upholstery. My mother saves and scrimps. But now they are in the Sheraton. The curtains pull smoothly across the rods. The swish of the fabric opens to a world of pavement and lights, of men teetering on bikes and women waiting for the bus. But for once my parents are above the world rather than inside of it. It is marvelous to see the man on the bike make a swift turn on Seventh Avenue while at the same time observing a woman dig in her purse for money as a bus, belching gray exhaust, approaches on West 52nd.

My mother stretches out on linens she hasn't had to launder. My father helps himself to a tiny bottle of scotch from the mini bar. The bottle is small and his hands are large, powerful, capable. They are in New York because my father has won the prestigious Allan Nevins Prize, given annually by the Society of American Historians to the author of the best written dissertation. They dress, my father in a tux and my mother in a lavender dress with a cord that cinches at her waist and sleeves that float, transparent, from the branches of her arms. They have no full length mirror in their Hyde Park apartment and this is the first chance my mother has had to truly study the shape of her belly, which hasn't really changed shape at all yet, but which she studies nonetheless. They take a cab to the dinner. There are speeches. There is the clinking of flatware. Centerpieces containing real flowers. The butter is cold and unspreadable. My father is given a certificate and a check for $1000. Under the table, my mother rolls bits of bread into tiny, pea-sized balls and then eats them surreptitiously. As her stomach rises up her throat she takes sips of water to push it down again. My father is so proud of winning the award he deserves. My mother is so proud she has not vomited on the table. They go back to the hotel then and my father says, *Let's go out, Rick, for a nightcap, to see the city. Let's really celebrate.* My mother shakes her head. She is exhausted and sick and wants to enter the deep sleep of early pregnancy that feels like a grave. *I'm going to go out, okay, Rick, just for a quick drink?* says my father. My mother rolls onto her right side. Closes her eyes. *Okay,* she says.

For my father, for half a block, the city throbs with life. Neon sizzles. Pigeons alight in a row on a bus stop bench. Each restaurant or bar spills a different combination of sound and scent onto the pavement, a combination he tries to identify as he passes through. A woman with spiked black hair and a cheek piercing tells him he's looking good. Men in long dress coats nod at him as though he knows their language. In the gutter, the sheen of oil is a beautiful, blotchy rainbow.

Then my father is pushed into an alley and robbed at gunpoint. The men take the cash in his wallet and then retreat, leaving my father unharmed but shaken. The half block back to the hotel throbs with a different kind of life, the raw and stripped down kind, life that takes at all costs because it wants to be born. The Sheraton elevator moves slowly and the pattern on the hotel carpet dizzies with its geometric repetition. My father crawls into the bed without undressing and closes his eyes. He doesn't wake my mother. He doesn't tell her what happened. He never tells her this story.

The bed is king-sized, which means my parents can sleep all night without touching, their worlds distinct and contained: my mother full of sickness and mystery, my father full of the $1000 he was given and the $20 he had taken away.

And I am somewhere in the middle, coming into being.

JANUARY

Reflection and Refraction

January begins beautifully. January begins with a dumping of fresh snow and the evergreen boughs in the Fireside Room still buoyant with good cheer. January begins with the hot cocoa machine fixed and enough power from the creek to use the clothes dryers occasionally. January begins with the taste of Christmas still in our mouths.

On Christmas Eve my mother and Peter invited most of the twenty-somethings (Miriam and Jeremy and Lucas and Aaron and Heather and Kent and me) up to their chalet. My mother distributed a small bottle of peppermint schnapps to each of us (green ribbon tied jauntily around the neck) and let us whisper and sing and sleep on their floor, a pile of un-washed limbs, our tongues dry, our sleeping bags tangled at our feet. The Christmas lights twinkled behind our closed lids. I slept with my head on Lucas's chest for most of the night, for the feel of flannel and the rise and fall of someone else's life below my cheek.

Then I went down the mountain and down the lake and over Sno-qualmie Pass to Seattle. The world had blossomed with flags. They were in the windows of stores, on the bumpers of trees, they were wrapped around tree trunks and fraying. I met my Intended at a coffee shop in the Univer-sity district. In the bathroom, before he arrived, I pinched my cheeks and pulled down the zipper on my REI fleece to just above my breastbone. In the coffee shop, taped to the glass pastry case, a tattered cut-out of Santa

Claus fluttered, holding a bag of gifts in one hand and a coffee mug in the other. From the overhead speakers came a jazzy version of "Santa Claus is Coming to Town."

I slipped my feet out of my winter clogs and put my wool-socked feet on the bench next to my Intended. He said "this chapter of our relationship is done but I don't think the book is over yet." I nodded as though I had been thinking the exact same thing. I took a sip of my mocha and let the whipped cream catch my nose so that I could delicately lick it off. Then he ran his thumb up the arroyo in the center of my foot and I thought *this loss is bearable, I just need to wait for the next part of our story to begin.*

January begins beautifully. Whereas usually the time following New Year's is dull and dreary, the emptiness of nothing to anticipate holding hands with the never-ending gray, a Holden January begins with a busload of college students from Pacific Lutheran University. The students are here to study ecology and theology and to observe the inner workings of an intentional community.

And the twenty-somethings of the village are thrilled to watch another group of twenty-somethings emerge from a bus. Because the community is small and relatively unchanging, because we are buried in snow, because the facial expressions and gestures of our fellow community members have become about as stimulating as bathroom wallpaper, everyone shows up for the arrival of the January term bus. We watch the frosted doors slide open and the students clomp down the stairs, their chatter quieting as they get their first glimpse of the mountains. A young woman with her hair wrapped into a crown of delicate braids follows a male student with two cameras around his neck, his dark hair stiff with gel. We watch their faces but also their clothes: scarves in bright colors with sparks of silver filigree, puffy down coats, and Guatemalan mittens. We observe their clothes but also their hair: light and clean, curled and soft. The fake fruity notes of their shampoo (lemon and pomegranate, grapefruit and cherry-almond) waft over to us where we wait, smiling and clapping, nodding our heads, saying "welcome, welcome." Ostensibly we are there to unload the food shipment, but more honestly we come out of a different kind of hunger: for the wider world and the sense of anonymity found there. We can't leave regularly so we find our own foreignness in the appearance of strangers who don't know us inside and out.

And, in the tradition of Holden, we play a lot of practical jokes on the January term students (aka J-termers) when they first arrive. We lead them in exercises to prevent flatulence; we play a game called Catch the Pony in which the entire village chases Finn in endless circles; we hook an exercise bike to the dishwasher and tell a student to pedal; we spend the first community meeting discussing whether the isolation of the men from the women has been successful. The J-termers get into the spirit and retaliate. They steal all the toilet paper from the common spaces, they mix cayenne into the Friday night brownies, they place cheese below a radiator in the dining hall and laugh when the entire room smells like athletic socks and dead mice.

We refuse to be outdone. Thursday lunch is hunger awareness. We usually eat potatoes or rice and send the money we save to a homeless shelter or sanctuary house. At the students' first hunger awareness meal we ask that the food be eaten in silence in order that we have ample time to reflect upon those we wish to help. Then we serve snow.

On their first Saturday night in the village, we hold a party for the J-termers in Lodge Six, mostly in Lucas's room. He plays techno music and everyone moves and shakes until they get warm enough to start taking off layers. The brightness of the overhead light is muted by a salmon-colored wall hanging. Along the walls Lucas has strung white Christmas lights, each covered in a tiny origami box, each box made from a differently patterned paper. On the bookshelf a tea light heats musky oil inside a small stone bowl. Someone has a bottle of rum. Someone has a bottle of gin. Miriam brings a pitcher of orange juice from the kitchen. The music is the same beat over and over again, twisting into different forms. Everything feels soft and blurry. People are dancing on Lucas's bed, people are making out in the hallway. "Let's take a shower," I hear someone say, and a few shadows slip out through the door. Lucas switches from techno to Jeff Buckley. I want to slow dance so I pull him to me. I put my hand beneath his shirt where his skin is soft and warm. I try to remember the last time I danced this way with my Intended but my mind is a maze and it spins. We run out of alcohol and Jeremy steals a box of the communion wine. Lucas's laugh is open and throaty, his lips are full and soft. The cigarettes he smokes make him slender and the bones on the crests of his shoulders feel like shells beneath his pale skin. I want to believe in something white and buried.

It is July 24, 1896. A man named J. H. Holden is deep in Railroad Creek valley, thighs wet with dew, hunting grouse beneath a sky marbled with clouds. He is hunting grouse but also ore. He is looking for the glint of sun on feathers but also the harder glint of sun on rock. He is listening for the purring cluck of the grouse but also for the silence of a mineral he feels has been calling to him since he came west twenty-two years ago. He is forty-one. He finds the ore.

J. H. Holden is clear about what happens next. Next will come investors, lining up at his door. Next will come a time of cigars and champagne and ease. But it is the spring of 1897 and no one wants to buy the ore. There is a nibble now and again. He takes interested parties up the lake to show them the ore. He washes the ore and places it in sunlight so that coming out of the forest the potential investors will be taken aback by the coy gleam. There is rumor down lake, in the town of Chelan, about what he's found. So J. H. Holden displays the largest piece of ore in the Chelan post office. Dull and rusty except for the side broken open that shows the furious sheen of the minerals inside. Holden likes to watch women, their arms full of packages, stop to gaze at it. One woman removes her gloves and touches the largest fleck of mineral with her thumb. Then she presses her thumb to her lips before returning her hands to her gloves. This woman becomes Holden's wife, Alma.

Or I imagine this woman was Alma. I like to think this is how Holden fell in love; when he saw his most fervent desire alive in another person.

On a Saturday in mid-January, we decide to hike to Big Creek. The "we" is my family plus Maggie and Bethany, two of the high school boarding students. Maggie, who is sponsored by my parents, has dark curls and Disney-sized blue eyes. She lives with my family in Chalet Six and my parents act like she is one of their own although most of the time Maggie acts like she doesn't want to belong to anyone. Maggie knows how to bake, how to bend reeds into baskets, and how to hem a curtain; but lately she's become obsessed with sewing a tent. After celebrating Christmas with her family on Whidbey Island, Maggie returned to the village with packages of blue silicone fabric and sturdy thread. She pinned images from Sierra Trading Post catalogs to her bulletin board and taped them along the bottom of her mirror.

Bethany's brown hair is cropped close to her round face. She's serious about schoolwork but she also jokes about an imaginary friend named

Billy whom she deems responsible for missing pencils and empty staplers in the classroom. As the winter progresses, Billy will become an honorary member of the high school class. His chair, like Elijah's, will remain empty and waiting. Bethany can kick a soccer ball further than any other woman in the village and her calculus homework, which I correct, is always neat and precise, the numbers and formulas descending down the graph paper in strict columns. Her laugh is a chuckle, warm and easy.

Big Creek isn't so much a creek as a valley, the basin formed between Copper mountain and Dumbell mountain and about two miles from the village. Though a round trip of four miles would be relatively easy in the summertime, four miles in the winter, mostly off trail and on snowshoes, is a full day trip. Big Creek is a slightly mythic place because it's only possible to reach it in the wintertime when snow has covered the alder and blackberry patches that make the way impassable in the summer months. It is a little like walking on water, this awareness that we are bypassing a world beneath. I wonder if Holden felt this way when he walked on solid ground, if he sensed the minerals slumbering, hungering to be released.

We stuff our day packs with Smart Wool socks, water, first aid kits, extra gloves, extra fleece jackets, space blankets, peanut M&Ms, and sandwiches of hummus and green pepper. My mother brings the silver whistle she's had since she lived in Hyde Park with my father. Peter brings a box of black licorice. I bring my journal and a pen. I have visions of sitting on a purple sleeping pad on an expanse of gleaming snow, composing poems that will be read around a heavy oak table by brilliant peers in an MFA program next year.

The day is cloudless and the snow, which has yet to be pockmarked with rain, is smooth and luxurious. We wear sunglasses, ostensibly to protect our eyes from the glare, but also perhaps because they give us all an aura of glamour and mystery. Because there are five of us we stop often: to adjust a snowshoe, to pee, to remove or add a layer of clothing, to take a picture of Michael who has found a fallen tree branch to use as a phallus. The first part of the hike is through evergreen and aspen, on a previously broken-in trail that we've hiked in the summer a thousand times.

Maggie and Peter take the lead, conscientious about direction and familiar with the spot at which we'll need to veer off the trail and down to a place where we can cross Railroad Creek. Michael hangs in the middle, head mostly down, ignoring the conversation before and behind him. His canary yellow jacket and his plodding and his disengagement are a kind of comfort to me. Bethany and my mom and I take up the rear, in part because we're less capable snowshoers and partly because we're chattering and laughing rather than saving all our breath and stamina for the task of lifting our feet, over and over and over again, through the loose powder.

Then we are out of the shadow of the trees and off the trail and winding our way down to the creek. The snow covers everything that is rough or sharp or spindly or scratchy in soft waves. If the sound of the word *ululation* were made into a landscape it would be this. Bethany and Maggie and I pose for a picture in between the glittering swells, our sunglasses raised and our eyes squinting into the sun.

We reach the creek, and more importantly the log that crosses the creek, a few minutes later and begin debating whether it's necessary to remove our snowshoes for the crossing. While Peter and Maggie assess the log, my mother begins a litany of "I don't know about this are you sure about this Peter please be careful Peter you're not thirty-five anymore please please be careful." Michael chucks craisins at my head and Bethany sits in a snow bank and laughs. It is eventually determined that Peter will remove his snowshoes and daypack and cross first. He edges to the end of the log and in that span of white, our four dark bodies quiet to watch him. In the wintertime this portion of the creek isn't fast or deep but it is still cold and wet. And we are at least a two-hour trudge from the village.

The log is covered in snow so Peter can't, from his vantage point, see the log itself, only the snow. And the snow itself has been blown to the east just slightly, just enough to form an eave that hangs over the edge of the log. This is what the rest of us notice just as Peter steps onto that eave: the promise of a way across when really, there is none.

In the summer of 1900, the Drummers Development Company entered into a ninety-day option agreement with James Henry Holden. They wanted to buy, they said, but they wanted ninety days to see if the mine was a viable financial prospect. Over the next three years, the DDC developed five tunnels, built a number of livable structures for the miners and the production staff (windows! piped water! a kitchen!), and graded twelve miles of mountain terrain in preparation for the railway that was to transport the ore from the mine to a barge waiting in the waters of Lake Chelan. But the capital requirements were prohibitive; in 1904, DDC backed out of the deal.

The few public photos from this era are grainy but seductive. Peering closer illuminates nothing; instead the figures and shapes become more fragmented, dividing into smudges, degrees of gray. The miners all look like slightly different versions of a single cast: dark work pants held up with suspenders, hats and buttoned shirts in various shades of dark and light. In one photo, taken in 1901, nineteen miners pose against a backdrop of evergreen and fir. The foreground of the picture is light, sun hitting the shale and dirt of the road. The slope of the mountain rises up the left side of the photo and a few of the miners sit or lean against the slope, maybe for the shade, maybe for the coolness of the stone. One miner, hands on thighs, sits above the others on an outcropping of rock, legs dangling. Another stands partway up the slope, gripping an overhang for balance. A boy-man in the center of the photo faces the mountain instead of the photographer, hammer propped on shoulder as though at a given cue he will swing into action. Another miner treats his pick like a cane, and a third holds his mining implement in his crossed arms, surly and protective. Their faces are practically invisible, darkened or lightened according to the quality and amount of facial hair; there is no easy way to enter this place. If you squint your eyes, the miners disappear, they have positioned themselves that close to the natural slope of the landscape. Their white shirts bleed into the sunlit shale, their pants marry themselves to shadow.

Four days have passed since the Big Creek trip. Peter fell through the eave of snow on the log and ended up with two wet legs. We pulled him out and dried him off as best we could. We gave him new Smart Wool socks and headed right back to the village. We didn't make it to Big Creek but Peter was okay. We were all okay and the way we told the story to everyone else made it into a comedy, a farce. "The log is right here" we kept saying, and laughing uproariously, repeating with glee Peter's last words before falling into the creek.

It's Thursday and I'm in the bathroom of the school, preparing for a science experiment with the elementary school girls later in the afternoon. They are studying light, reflection and refraction, so I am turning the bathroom into a pinhole camera. I am using my shoulder to press cardboard up against the window while simultaneously trying to remove a piece of duct tape from the roll when Christine, the elementary teacher appears in the doorway.

"You can set that down," she says.

"That's okay," I say, "I've almost got it."

"Here," she says, holding the cardboard in place while I secure it with duct tape.

"There," I say. "All done." Christine does not look particularly enthusiastic.

"Kaethe," she says, "Kent is here. From the kitchen," she says, as though I don't know which Kent she's talking about. "Kaethe, your mom has had an accident."

"What happened?" I should ask. But I am already out the door of the bathroom, I am already at the front door of the school, I am already pulling on my boots. Kent stands, glum and waiting. Christine hands me my coat.

"What happened?" I finally say to Kent as we walk out the door.

"She fell."

"Where?"

"Down the dining hall steps."

"Is it bad?"

"She's in pain. But she's going to be okay." Kent doesn't look at me but he puts his arm through mine and guides me down the road to the dining hall.

Just outside the eating area of the dining hall is a small area with a bathroom and a few offices. This is where the First Response Team has set up a station. They've hung a wool blanket from the doorway to prevent every member of the community from offering simultaneous support. My mother is lying on a cot. Sally, the village artist, is whispering into a walkie-talkie, and from one of the offices I can hear Gregory, the operations manager, asking the Forest Service to send a boat. I squat by the cot and take my mother's hand. When I lean toward her to kiss her cheek I smell Jergen's lotion and the West African Peanut soup the cooks are making for lunch.

"Just put a bullet in my head right now," says my mother.

"What?" I say.

"A bullet," says my mother. "In my head."

"Mom, you're going to be okay."

"No," she says, "I'm not. I'm going to have to limp around for months. I'm going to be a cripple. I'd rather be dead."

"You don't really want to die," I say. "You're just in pain. I understand."

"No, you don't," she says. "This happens to me all the time. Every winter I sprain my ankle or wrench my back and I'm just sick of it. I'd rather be dead." She turns her head away from me.

Gregory drives the wheelchair accessible van (the vehicle deemed to be the least bouncy) to the loading dock just outside the dining hall. The problem is how to transport my mother from the dining hall to the van. The cot on which she's currently resting won't comfortably fit through the dining hall doorways and any route will require passage over the lumpy, foot-wide trails of packed snow that criss-cross the village. Someone finally decides that my mother should be transported via chair.

My mother is horrified. "It's icy out there. It's icy. What if they drop me? What if they slip? They're going to slip. Don't let them do this. Don't let them do it. It isn't safe. It can't possibly be safe. Please don't let them do this."

Peter and I mumble some words of comfort.

Meanwhile, the seventy identical chairs in the dining hall are surveyed for sturdiness. All the chairs are leftover from the mining days. All are made of steel soldered around a seat the size of a dinner plate. All feature chipped paint and wobbly legs. My mother is right to be wary.

Jeremy and Finn are chosen to hoist my mother, on the chair, onto their shoulders. The rest of the village follows before and behind, my mother above us, a dark version of the Hora wedding dance. But my mother's face is not flushed and jubilant, it is frozen and blank. Her purple knit hat hangs slightly off-kilter and her heavy black winter boots (the ones designed to survive anything) dangle in the open air. Her thin, knobby hands clutch the seat of the chair, white with effort. I try to make eye contact but she won't look at me. A cheer erupts from the rest of the villagers when Jeremy and Finn reach the van and gallantly kiss my mother's cheeks. She nods and looks away. Peter gets into the van behind her and I stand, holding Michael's hand, as the door closes and her face disappears. Out of habit we wave until the van vanishes and then Michael and I turn and walk back to the school together without talking.

Christine encourages me to take the rest of the day off but I refuse, choosing distraction over worry. The elementary girls, Danielle, Johanna, and Natalie, all squeeze into the bathroom with me. We stuff a blanket below the crack in the door and I make a tiny hole in the cardboard window covering using a ball point pen. Then we turn toward the opposite wall. We stare at the blank space between the standard-issue mirror and the toilet with the seat that shifts slightly to the right when sat upon. We stare without talking until the world appears, upside down and blurry, three stripes of muted color: the brown road at head level, the stipple of pine trees at our feet and a white band of snow in between. I can smell the mustiness of the brown towels in the white metal dispenser and the skin heat of the girls (not the dank, musty smell of adult sweat but the potency of the world absorbed and returned through their skin). We hear a laugh from the high school room. From the elementary room comes the sound of Forrest jumping and Tasha counting "One, two, three, four . . ." Natalie leans a little over her right hip, crosses her arms over her belly. Johanna blows upward to sweep her bangs out of her eyes. Danielle says, "It's upside down, right? That's the road?"

I don't know anything about reflection and refraction so I don't know what questions to ask, what I should be coaching them to observe. I only know what they know: that the image is blurry and upside down, that the truth of the world has somehow been reversed via a tiny hole in a piece of cardboard. I turn on the light.

In 1905, Spokane mining industrialist J. P. Graves leased the Holden mine and gave J. H. Holden $5,000 to pay off bank loans and personal debt. Between 1905 and 1913, work on the mine intensified. The crew grew to thirty men who worked through the bitter, as well as temperate, months. Diamond drills were used to probe the exterior of the claim for further evidence of ore while inside the mountain the tunnels increased to five hundred then nine hundred then fourteen feet in length. A photo from that time shows a group of miners posed around an ore cart, the tunnel a prehistoric womb, the cart tracks stretching out into the lap of the viewer. It is an exercise in perspective and light: the tracks, shale, and cart in the foreground blasted white with the photographer's bulb. The two miners closest to the cart are also illuminated but the men behind them are less distinct and behind them the bodies blur until it is impossible to know whether the blackness at the vanishing point is made up of men or rock or emptiness.

My mother returns to the village one week later with a broken tailbone, a large supply of pain medication, and the anger of an active woman who has been told she must be still for the next two weeks. For the most part she stays in her chalet. We take turns pulling her to meals and Vespers on a purple plastic sled.

After two weeks she graduates to crutches. Attached to the rubber nubs of the crutches are sharp metal teeth. The marks the teeth leave in the snow look like the footprints of strange birds or like small, disfigured stars.

I begin to wake in the middle of the night. Sometimes I wake because of a roofalanche. The snow collects and grows heavy and then slides from the roof all at once. Because I live in the attic, my bed shakes as though I am inside a clap of thunder. When I wake I think of bombs, of fighter jets tearing open the sky.

Toward the end of the month I wake because of the full moon. Its brightness fills my room, not just its beams directly but also the reflection of its light on the snow below. It is eerie to be woken by the moon, a strange kind of calling I don't know how to answer. By morning clouds have arrived to cover the sun. The day is a dimmer version of the night.

Sometimes I wake because Lucas is in my bed with me and he moves or coughs or calls out in his sleep. I study his profile or his sharp Adam's apple, or the shallow divot in the middle of his chest, as though God had laid down her coffee spoon just so. I want to fall in love with Lucas, want to start a new chapter that doesn't feature the Intended, but my heart balks and burrows, won't be convinced. I keep thinking that in a day or two, in a week or a month I will be ready, that huge flowers will bloom along my neck and arms where Lucas touches me, that he will grow a tin can in his heart and I will grow a tin can in my heart and our hearts will communicate secretly, even when we aren't with each other, our golden words coiling around an invisible string.

By 1931 it was clear that there would be detritus produced in the process of separating the minerals from the ore and it was clear that something would need to be done with this detritus.

Someone proposed, because most of the minerals weren't "dangerous" unless exposed to air, running the tailings all the way down the mountain and letting them settle at the bottom of Lake Chelan. Others proposed a holding pond. But this proposition required the tailings to be stored mere feet from where the miners and their families lived, in the middle of a relatively untouched ecosystem.

In July of 1931, tailing samples were sent to H. A. Pearse, a mettalurgist by trade, to determine their potential environmental impact on Railroad Creek valley. Pearse constructed two glass tanks. In one tank the water was clear, neutral, controlled. Into the other tank he spun contaminated tailing water, the same concentration and composition found at the Holden mine. Both tanks also contained fish. The rate at which the fish died would mean something.

At the end of the summer Pearse sent his findings to the superintendent of the mine: "Although the fish in both tanks gradually died off, the loss in the contaminated tank was not appreciatively higher than in the tank which was supplied with fresh water only."

Not "appreciatively higher" meant, to the superintendent of the mine, "safe." Or safe enough. A tailings pond was constructed along the bank of Railroad Creek. Seven years later, the tailings dike broke. The water in the creek, from the mine down to Lake Chelan, was deemed unsafe. Still, the state did nothing to stop the production of the ore.

It's dark and cold. Friday night. It's not snowing so the stars are nicks to the heart. We're on the porch of Chalet Three, Lucas and Kent and Jeshua and Jeremy and Miriam and me. Kent has a banjo and Jeshua a guitar and they are singing bluegrass, songs that repeat a line again and again, the verse shifting the words slightly, but songs that say again and again, we are here, please listen, we are here. Lucas and I sit on the porch swing, cushions with exposed foam under our bottoms and a quilt stained with beer over our knees. This porch is off limits for smoking but I can smell the ash and sand from the yellow butt can on the rickety table in front of us, I can hear the crackling as Lucas rolls the tobacco together in his cigarette.

This porch is long and narrow, all of us facing the same direction except for Kent who sits on the railing with his banjo, facing us. We gaze out over the snow to the dining hall and beyond the dining hall to the place where the gray mountains hold a bowl of black between them. "There are angels hovering round," sing Kent and Jeshua, "there are angels hovering round."

The January term students left today. The pre-departure hugs went on for twenty minutes. Tears were shed. Fierce kisses blown from the bus windows. Many of the villagers and many of the students held scraps of paper with hastily scrawled addresses and phone numbers. The night before, at Vespers, many of the students said how devastated they were to go, how vastly they'd been changed by their visit. And we were sad to see them go. In part because we will miss their individual personalities but mostly because the village suddenly feels deflated, flayed down to its very bones.

The students will ride the boat and then a bus back to civilization. They will walk into malls and restaurants, they will walk into grocery stores and churches, they will walk down city streets and boardwalks and no one will know them. They will wake tomorrow and choose which version of themselves to present to the world.

"Shit," says Lucas, laughing, "that's the bread."

I smell it too. From far away, the scent of burning. Not exactly burning, but char, the scent of an object heated into black chemical residue.

"That's the bread I forgot to serve with dinner."

"Bet it's done now," says Jeremy.

"I'll help," says Miriam.

Lucas and Miriam trudge away from us, their figures dim until they swing the doors of the dining hall open and become briefly illuminated in the warm light. "I am a poor, wayfaring stranger," sings Kent, "traveling through this world of woe." Jeremy exhales a thin stream of smoke. I pull bits of stuffing from the cushion and line the bits up like breadcrumbs on the porch railing.

Then Lucas and Miriam are back again, each carrying a loaf pan filled with the burnt bread. Jeremy finds a walking stick leaning against the porch wall and meets them in the road in front of the chalet. "Pitch them to me," he says. And they do, as if they were expecting this, as if they brought the charred loaves over for this purpose exactly.

Kent and Jeshua stop playing then and though we can barely see, we watch the shadows of the charred bread float through the air like bats. January ends with the sound of that bread breaking. January ends with not a shattering but an emptying. January ends with the sound of puncture, with the whoosh of absence and release.

FEBRUARY

Litany of the Middle

Imagine this. The morning is cold and foggy in the small town where you live. On your way downtown in your heatless Honda you are stopped by the blinking red light and descending arm of the railroad-crossing signal. By the time you put your car in park the train is already rushing by, boxcar after boxcar, some peppered with graffiti, some flaking rust and paint, some stenciled with the name of an unfamiliar company. Fog obscures the engine and the caboose; there are only these cars in front of you, endless repetition with slight variation, on and on in front of your cold and silent car. This, to me, is February in the village.

The future blurs, refuses shape or form. I sent off applications to MFA programs in January but I won't hear any news until March or April. When I leave Holden in June, I could be moving to Colorado or Iowa or Montana or Oregon; I could be unemployed. The past is beginning to blur too: the previous year in California with my Intended, what it was we fought about, the exact arrangement of his features when we said goodbye. My mind has spent so much of the last months combing and re-combing the details of our time together that now each of the moments I return to seems frozen and lifeless. Untouchable. Now it's the unsought memories that make me catch my breath: the warmth of the outdoor heaters at our favorite Italian restaurant, a bastion of purple flowers entwined in a chain link fence, mango-vanilla iced tea sipped at a wrought iron table. Many of these newly

51

recalled memories don't even contain my Intended; I can't recall the past in the way I desire. There is only really this present, and though I know that time must be moving forward, February feels like a single day repeating itself endlessly.

My vision of myself is no different. Because there are no full-length mirrors in the village, I have to stand on a chair in order to see my body. And then the vision I get is truncated, shoulders to knees reflected in murky light, my own beginning and end outside the frame of what I can see. And it isn't just me that feels this way, it's all of us, our motions and routines rubbed so familiar that we have become threadbare and shabby.

I slip into Lucas's bed and he slips into mine. Miriam slips into Jeremy's bed and sometimes I slip into Jeremy's bed too, but only for warmth and breath, never for sex. Sometimes Heather slips into Aaron's bed but by the time she slips out again she is sad and Aaron is stony-faced. Kent composes in his bed and between antiphons writes letters to his girlfriend in Germany. My mother walks gingerly everywhere, angry that she has to walk gingerly everywhere and Peter curses about the cold, his phrases familiar as sung refrains. All of us hate oatmeal, hate snow, hate the cold that comes when we push the covers back because another day of the same is upon us.

At one end of the dining hall is a small map of the village and surrounding trails. Beside the map are little flags, red and green and yellow, that can be adhered to the map to indicate the avalanche danger along certain routes. Right now the only color on the map is red. Everything is poised to slide and so everyone is stuck here in the middle, repeating and repeating until the mountains let us go.

During the first weekend in February the village hosts a women's retreat. On Friday, fourteen women between the ages of forty-five and sixty-five emerge from the bus, most of them mildly overweight, all of them looking a little despondent and a little hopeful. One of the women, Elizabeth, is the mother of a friend of mine. I give her a hug when she emerges from the bus and I help her haul her luggage up the stairs to the dining hall. During lunch we listen to the other women as they exclaim joyfully over the homemade bread and black bean soup. After the other women retire to their rooms to unpack flannel nightshirts and anti-aging creams, Elizabeth and I walk over to the wall that houses the glass jars of tea. She asks me how I am.

I squeeze together the handles of my tea strainer to open the silver bulb at the end. I tell her about the breakup, about how I cry every day, about how the cold and snow and gray just keep repeating themselves. I bury the jaws of the strainer in a pile of Moroccan mint and then release the handles. "I know I sound cheesy," I say, "I'm full of all the clichés. But really, I can't stop crying." My throat constricts around the last words as though my body is trying to prove the truth of what I'm saying.

Elizabeth nods and pushes her glasses up the bridge of her nose. We run hot water into our cups. Stray flakes of tea float to the surface. "I went through a divorce," she says. "It took me three years to properly grieve that relationship." She opens the lid of the honey jar with her thumb and holds the jar above her mug. We both watch the amber take its time sliding down the glass. If we were anywhere else we would keep talking as she poured. When an ample amount of honey has finally slid into her mug she puts down the jar and stirs the tea. Then she turns her gaze to me again.

"Here is what I learned: I'm an Easter woman. I believe in the resurrection, sure, but I also believe in the tomb. I believe that darkness is crucial to the story. Do you understand?" I nod. I take a sip of the tea and feel a stray leaf catch on the inside of my lip. "You're in the tomb," she tells me, "so look around. See what it has to offer. You won't be here forever."

For the rest of the day I keep repeating Elizabeth's words in my head. I know she's right and at a rational level I know I should live though the darkness. But the truth is that I don't know how to do so gracefully. I imagine that moving one's way gracefully through darkness looks much like what the middle-aged women are up to this week: sharing stories of grief in a circle, lighting candles to commemorate the loss of this or that, walking the snowy labyrinth at the end of the road, carving phrases like "coming to terms with" and "breathing through" and "finding a space for" in battered journals. I imagine their grief is sober and sincere. But I am not a graceful griever. So instead I fill a Nalgene bottle with red wine and invite Lucas and Aaron down to the pool hall.

The pool hall is underground, in the basement of the village Center, and in the summer, as you walk down the stairs (leaving behind the heat of the dusty road and the cottonwood leaves turning silver in the sun) you can feel the coolness of the ground swallow you as you descend. The floor is gray cement. The main hall is filled with four pool tables, two with green felt, two with brown. A room at the end of the hall contains two smaller pool tables, a foosball table and a ping pong table. In another hall, parallel to the one that contains the pool tables, is the bowling alley. Four lanes, all slightly warped. Two rows of wooden stadium seats bolted to the floor. As a teenager, I loved setting the bowling pins: the surprising weight of each and the dark scars on the wood that the regular bowlers would never have the privilege of seeing. I liked laying the pins at an angle, each in its own slot, in the huge horizontal pyramid. I liked pulling the chain and watching the machine lower and then tip the pins upright, some teetering slightly as the machine retreated. I liked hopping onto the ledge behind the pit and squeezing my legs to my chest, liked feeling the force of a strike in the reverberations between my chin and kneecaps, the pins a white flash of total chaos and violence. I liked being that close, watching it happen again and again.

Whereas in the summer the coolness of the pool hall is relief, in the winter it's simply a deterrent. We dress in layers: long underwear below our pants, two or three poly-blend shirts below our thick wool sweaters. I wear a purple and fuscia beret that I crocheted last week; Lucas's green bandana is tied tightly over his greasy hair. Aaron sports a knit cap that says "Spicy" across the brim and features bottles of spices around the circumference. I've brought the wine and my battery-powered CD player. Aaron puts on Leonard Cohen and Lucas racks the balls.

"You guys play the first game," I say.

"Can we depend on you to keep the wine company while we play?" asks Aaron.

Lucas hands a cube of blue chalk to Aaron. "Break?"

The click of the balls sounds cold, sounds like glass or ice. The scent of popcorn and shoe spray and old paper lingers at the edge of things. Leonard Cohen sings about King David and secret chords. I stroll around the room, taking sips from the Nalgene, coughing loudly just as Lucas or Aaron attempt a difficult shot.

Around the outskirts of the main hall, on metal tables with chipping paint, are artifacts from the mine, rusting and labeled incorrectly (a bed pan is a "special instrument used in mining band" and a small wheel and axle are "cooking implement miners used for mashed potatoes.") On the wall are news clippings and photos and postcards, some ridiculous, some attempting a sort of nostalgia. The story of how Wes Prieb came to acquire

Holden Village for the Lutheran church (*Seattle Times*, 1960) is framed beside a postcard that advertises squeezable bacon. Beside a list titled "Ole and Lena's Favorite Pastimes" is a black and white photo of a dance in the village Center, circa 1949. The people in the photo look happy, like they don't realize they're living in the middle of the wilderness, like they don't feel the days repeating into infinity.

"Eight ball, corner pocket," says Lucas.

"Don't choke," says Aaron.

I walk over to the pocket in question and gyrate my hips a little. Then I shimmy my breasts, though the movement is barely noticeable underneath my wool sweater. Lucas rolls his eyes.

"It's like watching an Antarctic stripper," says Aaron.

I pout sadly. "Such cruelty. When I have the wine. Unwise."

The eight ball slips into the pocket. The cue ball slips in behind it.

"I win!" declares Aaron.

"Rematch," sighs Lucas.

I take another sip of wine and hand the bottle to Aaron. Cohen fills the room with images of Bathsheba and moonlight and marble. I turn back to the photo.

It is Christmas Eve, circa 1949. The village is buried under two hundred inches of snow. The flakes are falling fast on the five lodges and fourteen chalets, on the school and first aid station, on the dining hall and the sheds that house hydrants and coils of hose. Inside the recreation hall, the gymnasium is warm, filled with the kind of perspiring humidity that makes memory blurry the following morning. Dozens of people fill the gymnasium, confetti on the shoulders of black suit coats, confetti in the loosening pin curls of the women. Heads tilt back, mouths open in laughs or guffaws. People touch each other the way they do at parties that wind into the night: a man clasps another man on the back of the arm, a woman cups her hand under a man's elbow. They are dancing but the movements are simply an opportunity for contact, no one knows the steps. The music is furious with joy, the horns bright as copper. In the corner is a Christmas tree. The floor is strewn with tinsel. The men are miners. The women are their wives.

During the day the men go half a mile, a mile, a mile and a half into the largest copper mine in the northwest. If they are single they live in the dormitory-style lodges. If they have families they live further down the road at a place called Winston camp. They own their houses outright. They choose the design, the furnishings, they order the food that nests in the cupboards. In 1956, when the mine closes, they will pack up what they can before their carefully chosen houses are burned to the ground.

But for now it is Christmas Eve. They aren't allowed to drink but some of the men keep small flasks in their breast pockets. The women have reapplied their bright red lipstick. The wives work all day to create a sense of community, to keep civic pride intact. There are bridge clubs and knitting clubs, meetings for Boy Scouts and Campfire Girls. There are luncheons served by women whose long white gloves pull over their arms like a second skin. There is a group who gathers weekly to design clothing for a set of dolls. They photograph the dolls below the glare of a desk lamp, the figures leaning back imperceptibly against a backdrop because they are unable to stand on their own: Queen of Sheba, Scottish Lass, Irish Colleen, Gibson Girl.

When there is a birth, a shower, a holiday party, invitations are sent, the looping script requesting a formal reply. When the people leave the village, usually twice a year, they dress to the nines. In front of the school buses that will take them down the winding road to the boat the women pose in long fur coats, their high heels sinking slightly into the snow.

And across the creek from the road, from the village where the people dance and eat and bowl, the tailing piles grow higher and higher until they become the tiers of an impossible birthday cake, become a part of the landscape the people understand as home.

"Your turn," says Aaron, poking me in the ass with a pool cue.

Lucas takes the Nalgene bottle out of my hands and unscrews the lid. "Sometimes I feel like we missed out on living in the village during its prime," he says.

"I know," I say, glancing at the laughing mouths of the women again, "they look so happy."

"Like they're actually getting laid on a regular basis," muses Aaron.

"Not the mining days," says Lucas, "I mean the seventies and early eighties. Look at this guy. He's having the time of his life." Lucas's gaze is fixed on a color photo next to a postcard of a jackalope. The photo shows a bearded man in a white t-shirt and bell-bottoms skiing down the side of a tailings pile. The orange dust creates a hazy film on either side of him and the look on his face is pure ecstasy. "No one is telling that dude that he can't play Christmas Carols during Advent."

Aaron takes a swig of the wine. "Or they did but he doesn't remember because he's clearly high out of his mind."

"It looks like an ad for Vail or Banff that some photographer developed incorrectly," I add.

"Maybe you should write a poem about that," says Aaron, only half-sarcastically.

"She's not writing anything until I kick her ass at pool," says Lucas.

Lucas breaks and then proceeds to keep his promise. But in the unending gray and white of the month, it is a relief to see that many colors, spreading and colliding, touching and disappearing with no hint of predictability. This particular game has never been played before and won't ever be played again. "Hallelujah," sings Leonard Cohen, "Hallelujah."

After we finish our game and collect our things, after we turn off the lights and climb the stairs and move out into the night, I crawl into Lucas's bed. We are gentle with each other; we are doing what our bodies want us to do. But whereas my relationship with my Intended has turned, in my memory, into only a passionate beginning and devastating ending, my relationship with Lucas seems to be comprised of only a temperate middle. A place to live because there is nowhere else to go.

At night, when I can't sleep, I write a litany of the middle of things in my head:

The belly, the spleen, the yolk.
The volcanic core, the Cadbury center, the 50-yard line.
Noon.
The layer of clothing that doesn't touch the skin and doesn't touch the air.
The axis, the nucleus, the nose.
The man suspended on the wire over Niagara Falls.
The hours between death and resurrection.
The stratosphere. The canopy layer. The midnight zone.
Kansas. Oklahoma. Missouri.
Middle age.
The yellow dotted line.
July 2nd.

We live beside the middle of the mountain. The tailings rise 150 feet into the air. Three separate levels of orange dust, hard and compressed along the top, shifting and unstable along the sides. As a child, I didn't understand how the tailings were different from the sand dunes near Lake Michigan. Skiing them, like the man in the pool hall photo, looked fun and less cold than regular winter sports. I avoided them only because my mother so vividly described the way a piece of rusty mining hardware, buried surreptitiously below the dust, might slice my foot and cause lock jaw, a condition that (I assumed) would render me unable to speak (essentially the most terrifying scenario I could imagine). But I wasn't alone in my understanding of the tailings as a science fiction novelty. Many of Holden's visitors saw the tailings the same way: as a fluke, an oddity, a place for silly recreation. This was in 1980, the year the idea of Superfund sites was invented. Although the National Environmental Protection Act had been around for ten years and Carson's *Silent Spring* for eighteen, most guests didn't want to understand that they were vacationing beside an enormous pile of chemical residue. The orange color of the tailings, a result of the oxidation of the chemicals when exposed to air, made them cartoonish, laughable.

By the mid-1990s, the reality of the problem was becoming more apparent. In 1996, the Washington State Department of Ecology measured the effects of the tailings on the bottom-dwelling invertebrate life in Railroad Creek. Per meter squared, the average number of benthic invertebrates in the creek above the mine was 3,130. Directly below the mine: fifty. Three miles down valley from the mine: 110. At Lake Chelan: 361. Not only were heavy metals polluting Railroad Creek, but there was the risk that when the next great earthquake struck, a vast majority of the tailings would slide directly into the creek. The angle of repose wasn't right, it needed softening. As awareness about the problems grew, ecologists and geologists tried everything to contain the damage: rip-rap, matting, gravel, vegetation. Nothing truly worked.

Now, in 2002, there is talk of a full-scale mine remediation. There is talk of building a barrier wall, of a huge water treatment facility; there is talk of regrading the tailings and capping the mine portal for good. But amid the talk is the recognition that these are the kind of solutions that help for two hundred years, not two thousand or two million. This is our version of remediation. We will heal the creek temporarily. We will stop the groundwater contamination temporarily. We will stop the tailing dust from whirling into the air and landing on the fur of rabbits, on the waxy glare of new cottonwood leaves, on the veined backs of elderly hands temporarily. Until the barrier wall breaks. Until the caps no longer hold. Until the angle of repose is no longer sufficient. And then the tailings will contaminate again. Because the truth is that although we can hinder the effects for awhile, we can't actually make what we've done go away. We created the beginning and we can predict the eventual end.

So what do we do with the middle? What can the middle of things—the sick insides of Copper Mountain, the darkness of the tomb, the temperate relationship, the gray days of February—what can these things give us? And how can we receive what they offer with any kind of grace?

I don't have an answer to any of these questions, but I know what Simone Weil might say. My father, dean of an honors college in Indiana, has limited knowledge of contemporary culture but a fairly agile understanding of many of the "great" thinkers (dead, white men—and occasionally women—whose intellectual acuity peaked before 1950). My father's main way to comfort his children in times of distress is to send us an article or book that, theoretically, contains a solution to the crisis in question. He sent me Kierkegaard for Christmas and, when that didn't seem to do the trick, Simone Weil. *Waiting for God* arrived a few days ago and I've been making my way through it slowly, coupling Weil's own words with the story of her life (via a battered biography in the Holden library). It's the details that fascinate me most: scars on her fingers from the button factory, ribs like corrugated tin from refusing to eat more than her fellow workers, headaches that stretched along her jaw and into the sockets of her eyes.

Thus far, my overall assessment is that she's brilliant—though I have the sneaking suspicion she'd be the woman at the party whose eyes would widen slightly in internal distress when you tossed your beer can into the trash instead of the recycling. Still, I'm caught by her fierce admonitions to pay attention since paying attention is how we practice sidling up to God. On an index card I write out my favorite quote in purple marker and pin it to my bulletin board: "One of the principal truths of Christianity, a truth that goes almost unrecognized today, is that looking is what saves us." The poems I love suggest this same practice, a watchfulness that eschews judgment. Though many of the most-beloved poems in the canon are about beginnings and endings, life and death; the best poets seem able to make a lived experience out of the middle of things too.

It's not difficult to pay attention when, on Monday, a large box arrives addressed to my mother. On Wednesday, another box. On Friday a third and a fourth.

When my mother fell down the stairs in January, she left an unfinished family Christmas letter behind. In a note from the hospital that began with "Honey" and ended with "please keep an eye on Michael" she requested that I finish the letter for her. Most people in our address book don't understand this village exactly and many think we may be part of a cult. So I used the letter writing as an opportunity to confirm their suspicions. I wrote about how we sacrifice goats and how Peter has taken up basket-weaving. I mentioned Michael's new relationship with Satan and my mother's accident and her intense desire for Harlequin romance novels. I underestimated the number of people on our Christmas list with no sense of humor and no sense of my mother's literary tastes.

The boxes are full of Harlequin romance novels. Lucas and Miriam take breaks from kitchen work to help me unpack the books. We drink press-pots of coffee and arrange the books according to cheesiest title, man with largest pectoral muscles, and woman with largest breasts. When my mom comes to dinner we always have one waiting on her plate. Sometimes I hide one below her pillow or below a pile of rags in one of the cleaning closets.

The books also solve a curricular dilemma. I am Michael's Spanish teacher and we have spent the year thus far using the textbook his Minneapolis high school sent with him to Holden. But recently we have become disgusted by the inherent class prejudice within it. Last week's vocabulary lesson included the words for *snorkeling, jet ski*, and *red snapper*. So when I discover *El Regalo Más Hermoso* among the English-language Harlequins, it becomes our new Spanish textbook.

Once a month Ben and Beth (village pastor and village hospitality manager, respectively) hold a gathering in their chalet called Wine, Chocolate, and Poetry. People bring as much of each item as they can, sometimes they simply bring themselves. Those who have recently been on an "out" are usually generous with provisions; sometimes there is even a block of expensive cheese or wasabi peas or sherry in addition to the wine. I bring most of the poetry books, from my own collection and from the small library in Koinonia. We sit in the living room of the chalet, on the couches and chairs, cross-legged or prone on the floor. There isn't any conversation once we begin, just one poem read after another. Sometimes silence in between, always the sound of pages being flipped, spines being cracked wider.

Tonight Heather brings artichoke dip. Jeremy stretches out in the dining room, his felt hat covering his eyes. There are ten of us in the room and it is warm with the heat of bodies and words spoken slowly enough that their worlds appear before us. Mark reads Whitman: "all goes onward and outward, nothing collapses"; Miriam reads Marilyn Hacker, desire creaking at the back of her throat. Lucas enters and stays for just ten minutes, leaning against the heavy oak door without taking off his boots. Aaron reads "Dickhead" by Tony Hoagland, about making a word his friend. The artichoke dip grows cold; maroon rings form on the coffee table; Jeremy begins to snore gently. I read one of my own poems, "the half sound of missals reminds us of our bodies / half bitten by mosquitoes/ who drone listless through the half-blue skies." Sometimes there are light murmurs or nods after a poem or laughter if it's funny, but never judgment of any kind, never commentary. Ben reads "The Lake of Innisfree" and we walk home with that landscape laid over our own: linnet's wings and bee hum above the steady silence of snow.

During the winter the only direct sunlight we receive occurs during the two hours when the sun travels between Buckskin and Copper Mountains. Because it's winter, the sun hangs low in the sky, sulking, never making it over the crests of the mountains, only passing behind. Sometime in late February, the sun gets up the gumption to loop a little higher and, for the first time in months, summits Buckskin and slides slowly down the other side. To celebrate, the village celebrates Sun Over Buckskin (or SOB) Day. School is cancelled. A parade is prepared. Everyone dresses in the brightest colors they can find: turquoise swim suits, magenta long johns, beach sarongs, clown wigs, yellow rain boots, rainbow-striped leg warmers. Everyone wears sunglasses and even the most stoic villagers succumb to Stella's offer to smear silver glitter paste on their cheekbones. The cooks prepare an outdoor barbeque on the road. Kent turns the burgers wearing a white tank top, red suspenders, and a child's inflatable water flotation device around his waist. When Kent bends toward the grill, the swan head of the toy bends too, so close to the fire I think it might pop or melt—but it doesn't.

Between events, Lucas and Miriam and Finn and Jeremy and I climb Chalet Hill to the uppermost chalet, number ten, vacated during the winter but with a porch blazed by the sun and a view of the village and valley. We drink beer and whiskey. Rest our legs on the railing of the porch, tilt back in our chairs, lift our faces to the sun.

We return to the road for SOB Day proclamations. I read a poem modeled after Pyramus's paean to the moon in *A Midsummer Night's Dream*: "Sweet Sun, we praise thee for thy brilliant blessed glittering gleams, for blistering now so bright." Kent and Jeshua sing "Here Comes the Sun." The students perform a synchronized swimming routine. Scott and Christine, the teachers, hold up a long, sky-blue tarp, wiggle it slightly so we know it's water. The students lay on their backs behind the tarp, raise their legs so their toes point toward the sky, and support their raised hips with their hands. A battery-powered stereo plays "I Will Survive" and the bare legs begin to bend and stretch, point and flex in rhythm to the music.

On the way back to chalet ten for more whiskey and beer and sunbathing, Jeremy pinches my ass, plants a kiss on Miriam's neck.

"Get a room," says Finn.

"Cigarette?" asks Lucas.

The winter feels surmountable.

At Vespers we're hungover. We lay under the dim lights in the balcony of the Fireside Room. We sing "For the Beauty of the Earth" and then we're invited to say one thing we witnessed today for which we want to give thanks. That's the whole service. Ten minutes of darkness and out of it, voices we recognize giving us back the day in portions, the mundane made holy with gratitude.

By February 26 I am no closer to knowing anything about my future. There has been no word from my Intended, no word from graduate schools, no approach of an angel to tell me what is meant to be. And I don't have any neat answers for what the tomb might offer me. I have learned how very human I become when there is no way out.

And then, sometime around 11 p.m. it happens. Distantly at first and then louder. We throw blankets over our shoulders and go out to stand on the road in the darkness. The snow is sliding, up the valley from our village but loud enough it sounds like the avalanches are descending upon us. One after another, world without end.

The next day the chart in the dining hall is filled with green flags instead of red ones. Jeremy and Miriam and I put on snowshoes and head up the valley. I always imagined an avalanche to be puffy and white, dangerous but pure somehow. When we near the first avalanche site, I see how wrong I've been. An avalanche is hungry, it digs things up. It carries with it not only snow, but anything else on the face of the mountain that is weak or weary or delicately attached. The avalanche pile is dirt and grime, is branches and boulders, is everything we forgot was below the snow. We climb the ruin and walk upon it, glad, momentarily, to be free.

MARCH

Vigil with Cougar and Sackbut

I love to be in the woods. But I am terrified of being in the woods alone. Specifically, I am afraid of being mauled by a bear (summer) or a cougar (winter). My fear is not entirely unfounded.

A few years ago, four of the junior high and high school village girls decided to walk, unsupervised, from the village to the lake. Thirteen miles is a long trip, but the road is plowed in the winter so the trip required boots rather than snowshoes, and promised a wide and direct route. The avalanche danger was low, no snow was predicted, and these girls were capable, savvy, and confident. They would leave in the early morning, hike down to the lake, and spend the night in an A-frame building that featured a wood stove and simple cots in addition to mice and soot. The next morning, the girls would ride the bus back up the mountain with the newly arrived guests. Their parents made sure the girls packed first aid kits and space blankets, extra layers of clothing and an avalanche shovel. Then the girls were given a walkie-talkie, which they named Guido, and set free.

About four miles down the road, as they walked in a happy line, eating bits of snow, and singing a rather compelling rendition of "Closer to Fine," they noticed a cougar approaching them from the opposite direction. These girls knew their stuff and they did all the right things. They waved their arms, they made noise, they held their packs above their heads in order to appear larger and more threatening. But this cougar was an adolescent, likely more curious then hungry, and so he continued his approach.

It is not uncommon, given the age of most Holden vehicles, for them to break down or need service en route from the village to the lake. So, wisely, the operations folk park spare vehicles along the road every few miles so that a stranded driver is always within walking distance of shelter and transportation.

The girls had passed just such a vehicle about fifty yards before they saw the cougar. So when their best efforts to intimidate the cougar failed, they began to back up together, still waving and yelling, until they reached the spare van. They hustled inside, slid shut the door, and turned on Guido. By this time the girls could no longer see the cougar but they were told to sit tight anyway until parental support arrived.

When, fifteen minutes later, the second van did arrive, the parents noticed the cougar, still curious and hungry, waiting patiently below the van while the girls ate granola bars and played hangman inside it.

Ironically, the cougar confrontation did nothing to change the relationship those girls had (and still have) with the woods. They went on being capable and savvy and confident. But I think of that cougar each time I move outside of the periphery of the village. I think of its slow and curious amble closer. And closer. And closer.

I think of the cougar when Lucas and I go galumphing out into new snow on a night in early March. The stars are sequins on velvet and the snow is sweet and light and up to our thighs. We trip and fall and laugh. We make snow angels and give them breasts and devil horns. The snow is too light to be formed into snowballs so we throw armfuls at one another, the flakes catching the moonlight in a gorgeous, fizzy mist that any romantic comedy would be proud to include in a winter love montage. Finally, we sink into cold and stare up at the sky while we catch our breath.

"Do you think moments like this one are balanced by moments of terror?" I say.

"What?" says Lucas.

"I'm just thinking about Afghanistan."

"Why are you thinking about Afghanistan right now?"

"I just wonder sometimes if the world is meant to be neutral, emotion wise. Not horrible, not lovely. And so there's always this teeter-totter thing in effect. If we're having a good moment then someone else is suffering.

And if I'm suffering then someone else is having great sex in a room full of rose petals and sunshine."

"That doesn't make any sense."

"I know," I sigh.

"I'm going to take a piss," says Lucas. He wades through twenty yards of snow and disappears behind a tree.

Maybe it's not so much that the ridiculous beauty and joy of this particular moment causes pain elsewhere in the world, but the moment does make me feel suddenly guilty. For the cleanliness of the snow. For silence and space and safety. I don't know what a Middle Eastern war zone feels like, but the version in my imagination is the direct opposite of this. And yet, here I am in the midst of a tremendous amount of safety, terrified of an invisible cougar slinking through the dark. Any decent self-help book would, I know, suggest that in order to move forward in my life, in order to rid myself of the constant psychic presence of the Intended, in order to grieve and release and move on, that I need to confront the fears that paralyze me in some way. "Eat the peach," this self-help book would say to Prufrock, "part your f-ing hair behind." It's time to force the moment to its crisis, it's time to catch the cougar by the tail.

Three days later, feeling decidedly less poetic, I waddle across the hallway and into Jeremy's room dressed in snow pants and down coat and boots. I tell Jeremy that I'm going out to the rock behind the school, the one beside Railroad Creek, and that if I'm not back in twenty minutes he should come looking. Jeremy, a wilderness first responder who enjoys solo ice climbing trips, looks up from his book and rolls his eyes at me.

"No. Seriously, Jeremy," I say.

"Fine," says Jeremy.

"Do you even have a clock in here?" I say.

"Nah," says Jeremy, "the one I borrowed from Koinonia broke."

Jeremy's property ethics have more to do with awareness and less to do with actual ownership. He believes that if he takes something and the person doesn't notice it's missing, then by all rights the item should be his since the person didn't care enough about the object to notice its absence. He gladly returns objects (when he can) if their presence is missed by the owner. Jeremy has gladly returned my scissors, my nail clipper, and a variety of thumb tacks and paper clips. But it is unlikely I will ever see certain squares of chocolate or slugs of wine or postcard stamps again. And that's okay. What I'm concerned about at this present moment is that Jeremy won't notice my absence for three or four hours by which time the cougar will be paw-painting with my blood.

"Here's my watch," I say in what I hope is a helpful rather than desperate tone. I set the timer for eighteen minutes and set it on his nightstand.

Jeremy doesn't look up from his book.

"The rock behind the school," I remind him.

Jeremy yawns.

I don't even make it to the rock. I make it to the exact spot where, behind a scrim of trees and a rounded shoulder of snow, the roof of the school disappears and I feel suddenly alone in the woods. I stand still and listen. There is the faint rushing of the creek—made fainter in the winter by the encroachment of snow and ice on the surface of the water—but above and beyond that sound there is nothing. Silence.

I just need to be here, to be present in the silence, I say to myself, trying to think like a middle-aged woman on retreat. I take a few deep breaths. I close my eyes. I open my eyes to check how much time has passed and then realize I left my watch with Jeremy. I sink into the snow and keep careful track of the cold as it progresses into my butt, my thighs, my lower back. I think of being found tomorrow, frozen to death in this exact spot. I cross my right leg over my left so that I will look jaunty and relaxed when they find me. I consider whether my Intended would come to the funeral. Of course he would come. Would he bring his new lover? My death might bring them closer together. They might have the best sex they have ever had because of my death. I sigh. I look for ice mites on the top of the snow.

I hum a little of "You Can't Always Get What You Want" but the sound is false and the moment I stop humming, the silence swallows everything again. Silence is supposed to be a refreshing balm but I find this silence oppressive. My ears strain, trying to catch the sound of snow falling from a branch or tiny claws skittering over bark. Nothing. The silence is a cavern. The silence is worse than a cougar.

I'm not exactly afraid of the silence. I'm afraid of who I am in the silence. Each relationship presents us with a natural role to play: daughter or student or friend, colleague or community member or lover. I know who to be, I know who I am when presented with a relationship. If the cougar appears, I will know who I am in that relationship. But alone, in the snow,

I realize that my real fear is that without others around, as foils or support, that maybe really I am nothing. Or nothing worth remembering.

The devout Christian might here remind me that I am a child of God. That at this moment I am still in relationship with a creator who knew me from the time she knit me in my mother's womb.

The Buddhist might say, "Exactly! You are nothing! But what freedom there is in emptiness."

And maybe both of these are true. But at the moment neither truth brings me comfort. I see instead a vision of myself with my identity on the outside, scale and armor, feather and fin. My outside to the world bright and showy but on the inside, where I should be able to find—what? I don't know exactly. The comfort of the soul, of the known, of my own good human potential? In this space—nothing.

This is not a new dilemma. It is the age-old human dilemma. But a personal encounter with one's own hollow center is no less devastating simply because others have a hollow center too. In fact, this makes it worse.

I take my hands out of my mittens and use my fingers to plug my ears until I hear the soft drumbeat of my own blood, until my breath comes like wind to save me.

After a long time, I heave myself up and wade through the snow back to the chalet.

"Nine minutes," says Jeremy, without looking up from his book, "nice work."

Luckily, I have a rejection letter in my mailbox to bolster my spirits. The MFA program in Oregon doesn't want me and coincidentally I have just decided that I am not so interested in them either. I tear the letter into tiny bits and dispose of it in the bio-waste container in the women's bathroom. Because we sort through all the village trash during garbology, the bio-waste containers (home to tampons and condoms and the like) are the only receptacles in the village where disposal is absolute.

After disposing of the letter I wash my hands and make some toast and head over to the community meeting in Koinonia. Luckily, there are no issues to be determined by consensus tonight so the meeting practically flies by. A mere seventy minutes into the meeting and already we have come to the final activity: pass-arounds. Pass-arounds are merely announcements that carry some need for written commitment. Miriam stands first and asks for volunteers to help make pancakes on Thursday morning. She holds up a clipboard as she speaks and hands it to the person next to her as she sits down.

John, our fire chief, stands up with an identical clipboard and asks for volunteers to adopt a hose house. There are nine hose houses in the village, tiny shacks containing two coils of hose, a hydrant, a gated wye, and a wrench. When the fire alarm in the village sounds, the first villager to the blinking alarm board picks up the microphone and announces in which building the alarm has sounded and to which hose house villagers should report. We all then trudge to that hose house and stand in a line, theoretically preparing ourselves to pull the hose if necessary, but actually shivering and chatting until the searchers check the designated building and call an "all clear." John is leaving the village for two weeks and wants to make sure the hose houses (and the paths leading to the hose houses) are kept free of snow while he's away. "I hope you'll all consider looking after a hose house," he says, handing the clipboard to Heather.

Finally Heidi, registrar and lay minister, stands with a third clipboard. "Easter comes early this year, everyone. March 31st. So it's time to begin preparing. For those of you who haven't been present for an Easter in the village, I want to explain a little bit about how things work.

"Although we will, of course, have a liturgy with holy communion on the 31st, the real celebration happens on the night of the 30th. The Easter Vigil will begin at 9pm outside the village Center where we will welcome God's promise of light. We'll then proceed into the village Center for the service of baptismal remembrance. The next part is where all of you come in," she says, tapping her pen against the clipboard she is just on the cusp of offering us. "During the next part of the vigil we'll progress around the village to different stations. At each station we'll hear a story from the Old Testament. A different committee will be in charge of each station and your group can decide where in the village you'd like to perform. The vigil will be long, maybe three hours, and so the point is to have fun with your story. Be creative. And yes, you can leave the vigil if you need to use the restroom or to warm up. We'll conclude in the Fireside Room around midnight where we'll celebrate the resurrection with communion. Then we'll head directly to the dining hall for a huge feast that the kitchen staff is already beginning to prepare."

When the sign-up clipboard comes to me I glance at the list (Noah's Ark, Jonah and the Whale, Abraham and Isaac, Valley of Dry Bones, etc.) and then sign up for The Fiery Furnace.

A few days later, our Fiery Furnace group meets in the Fireside Room to plan our skit. My mother is part of the group as is my brother, Michael, and Stella, postmistress and glitter queen extraordinaire. The other members of the group are Eric and Andrew. Eric, a member of the village operations crew, is tall and handsome with a curly blond beard and a degree in engineering. Andrew is the tech support person in the village. Glasses and a shock of blond hair frame Andrew's face. Regardless of the season, Andrew struggles with sinus issues and wears a windbreaker.

We begin by reading chapter 3 in the book of Daniel together. The mighty ruler of Babylon, King Nebuchadnezzer, made an image of gold and demanded that everyone in his purview worship the image. Specifically, he commanded that anytime anyone heard the sounds of the "cornet, flute, harp, sackbut, psalters, [and] dulcimer," those people should fall down before the golden image. Shadrach, Meshach, and Abednego refused. King Nebuchadzezzer threatened to throw the men into a fiery furnace if they did not worship the image. Still, Shadrach, Meshach, and Abednego refused. So the King cranked the furnace up to "seven times more than it was wont to be heated" and had the rebels tossed inside. Shadrach, Meshach, and Abednego did not burn. When the King peered inside the furnace, he saw not only the flame-resistant rebels, but also a figure that looked to him like the Son of God. King Nebuchadnezzer called Shadrach, Meshach, and Abednego out of the furnace and proclaimed they need not worship any god other than their own.

It takes us quite awhile to make it through the story, in part because the names of the characters don't exactly roll off the tongue and in part because the litany of "cornet, flute, harp, sackbut, psaltery, dulcimer" is repeated four times in the first fifteen verses.

"What the hell is a sackbut?" Stella asks when we finally finish reading. All of us shrug.

"Sackbut," says Michael, poking me with his foot.

"It takes a sackbut to know a sackbut," I say, poking him back.

"I'll be the king," says Andrew, pulling his windbreaker tighter.

"I'll build something to light on fire," says Eric.

"I'll work on a script," I say.

My mother raises her hand. "I'll help."

"And I have gold lamé pants, says Stella, "so I can be the statue they worship."

We all turn to Michael. "I'll find a sackbut," he says.

We agree to meet in two weeks, on Good Friday, to practice.

The bus is pulling up at the loading dock as I leave the meeting. I hug Jeremy and Lucas as they emerge. They've been gone only forty-eight hours, mostly for the purpose of procuring booze for a St. Patrick's Day Party. They head into the dining hall to eat lunch with a few new guests who have arrived with them on the bus, and I join twenty or so other villagers in the unloading line. We stand staggered, facing one another, and pass the packages up: snug, sealed boxes of butter, flats of eggs, and unwieldy cartons of bananas, the fruit ripe enough that we can smell the scent through the holes in the box. Luggage, the airline tags still sticky; a Styrofoam cooler filled with salmon and a plastic cooler filled with gallons of ice cream. The corner of one box is mushy and my fingers slip through the mealy cardboard. There isn't enough sawdust on the snow path below our feet and I wrench my back, slightly, while pivoting with a bag of flour. When the container is *heavy* or *fragile* we call out the word and it travels up the line like a slightly dysfunctional echo. As I heft three boxes covered with Lucas's initials, I smile at the sound of bottles tinkling inside. Last come the bags of mail and the red pouch, zippered and glossy, filled with phone and e-mail messages from the bed and breakfast down lake. Work orders, flight confirmations, updates on Uncle Ralph's surgery, all the paper slips get pinned to a bulletin board outside the registration office with the recipient's name scrawled across the outside.

While we wait for the mail to be sorted, Kent and I attempt our first musical collaboration. Because everyone in the village loves an excuse to dress up, the twenty-somethings have decided to make the upcoming St. Patrick's Day party into a wake for an invented persona named Patrick McBlarney. All party-goers have been encouraged to dress as a friend or relative of Patrick, and Kent and I have been charged with writing a drinking ballad to commemorate Patrick's untimely death. By the time Stella comes whistling through the dining hall with the empty mailbags under her arm we have a refrain:

> Patrick McBlarney, Patrick McBlarney
> A noble friend so true.
> Patrick McBlarney, Patrick McBlarney
> We raise this glass to you.

The rejection letter I receive in my mailbox from Minnesota inspires me to go home and write a few more verses. By dinnertime I've helped Jeremy test the potency of his newly procured Jameson whiskey and conceived of an arc to Patrick's life, beginning with a nurse "slapping his quiv'ring arse" and ending with his bathtub suicide over sexual performance issues.

The next day comes and it's gray. It rains. The snow becomes a sharp crust. I spill my coffee and I don't get invited to a gathering in Chalet Five that involves Heather's artichoke dip and good gossip about village happenings. Desire seeps out of my body and crawling into Lucas's bed, summoning the energy to become aroused feels like work instead of instinct, like pulling a sled up a hill instead of coasting down a slope, unimpeded. Another rejection comes and then another. I read, again and again, a poem by Tony Hoagland called "Adam and Eve." I write out my favorite stanza on an index card and tape it to my mirror:

> I've seen rain turn into snow then back to rain,
> and I've seen making love turn into fucking
> then back to making love,
> and no one covered up their faces out of shame,
> no one rose and walked into the lonely maw of night.

Except I do want to cover up my face and I do walk out into the lonely maw of night. I am tired of being in the middle, in the liminal space, of my wheels spinning and spinning in the dissolving snow. I'm not the only one who feels this way; the fact that we are edging towards spring doesn't make the bleakness easier, in many ways it makes it worse. Appropriately, on the 16th of March, a Saturday, all of us have a wake to attend.

It turns out Patrick McBlarney has three wives. A husband. Two drunk uncles. A twin sister who might be a lover. A pool boy, a broker, a personal brewer. His mother wears a green kerchief and pearls. Jackie O. sunglasses. She drowns her sorrow, as we all do, in drink.

The party takes place in a room called the Lift. It's a dingy dark room the miners used as a bar (sans the prohibited alcohol). Up front is a small wooden stage with a piano. A wooden bench runs along the back of the room. To the left of the stage are two booths. Between the benches of the booths hang tables from wrought iron chains. Each link on the chain is the length of an open hand. Above the booths and the long wooden bench is a lofted area that can be reached by climbing a thin metal ladder. On the other side of the stage is a small galley kitchen with an old sink, a stereo, and a small light board for operating the three spotlights that hang above the stage. In the summer there's a talent show on the stage every Friday night and people pile into the room with ice cream and popcorn and plastic glasses filled with Coke. Kids dangle their legs off the side of the loft and from below they make the room look alive, tentacled. If you sit in the unheated room alone for long enough you can hear the mice skittering across the floor.

Midway through the party Aaron decides the bathroom is too far away. He uses a plastic bucket in the little galley kitchen instead. The Guinness disappears. Then the hard cider. By midnight we are down to only the Jameson. By midnight, too drunk to care about the seven verses, we simply sing the refrain of the drinking song over and over again. The more we sing and the more we drink, the truer the song becomes.

Patrick McBlarney, Patrick McBlarney
A noble friend so true.
Patrick McBlarney, Patrick McBlarney
We raise this glass to you.

At midnight Lucas catches my eye from across the room. He raises his eyebrows and smiles. I turn away. When I look again, he's gone.

At two in the morning Jeremy finds me in a nest I have fashioned out of all the down coats. "Let's get you home, poetessa," he whispers.

In the bedroom mirror my image sways. The Tony Hoagland quote blurs. I lean closer and notice the imprint of the grains of wood from the loft imbedded into the smooth flush of my cheek.

I spend the next morning, a Sunday, trying to write my way through a hangover. I sit in the dining hall and alternate between coffee and water. Lucas tosses me an orange but doesn't come over to talk. Jeremy laughs at me. Miriam suggests I make an appointment with Dee Dee.

Dee Dee is sixty-ish and wears jeans, thick sweaters, and muk-luk boots. She's not Christian, not even vaguely, but she believes in fate and energy. Her hair is long, brown, and brittle. She is always trying to purge her body of something and her diets make her skin smell like apple juice with a hint of bitterness behind. A potent sweetness. Dee Dee lives at Holden with her husband because they love the quiet and isolation and because both of them were having trouble finding work at home. She is teaching herself Reiki and has offered to practice on members of the village.

I trudge up to her chalet after lunch and stretch myself out on her couch. She has just made tea and the small room is warm and moist from the steam. She opens a spiral bound manual and sits down beside me, tells me to close my eyes. "The purpose of Reiki," she explains, "is to get the energy moving smoothly through the body. Sometimes it gets stuck. Like a stream getting mucked up with sticks and leaves. I'm just gently reminding the water of its natural passage."

She rests her slim fingers on me: right hand on my leg and left hand on my shoulder, then right hand on my wrist and left hand on my chest, then right hand on my temple and left hand on my hip. I drift off into images. A red hot air balloon. The glistening belly of a trout. Soft ivory slippers in the shadow of a bed. From time to time I feel just her left hand on me while her right hand turns the pages of the manual. I don't know if she's healing me or even curing my hangover, but I am grateful for hands that touch my body without wanting anything in return.

A week and a half drags by and it's Maundy Thursday. As we enter the Fireside Room for Vespers, it's already there: the quiet, the pall, the known ending of this story smoking a blue cigarette in the corner.

I walk up to the balcony and lay on my belly, propped on my elbows. On the main floor across from me, in front of a triptych covered in purple cloth, five or six villagers shuffle white pages and adjust black music stands and clip-on reading lights. Because the Vigil will be so long on Saturday, the worship planning committee has decided to combine the Maundy Thursday service with story of Christ's passion (usually read on Good Friday). I don't really know what this means liturgically except that we're in for a really long Vespers service. The ring of stones in the center of the room features two scarlet table runners and a large Bible. At the very center, in the shallow bed of sand, four white tapered candles surround a metal cross. The light dives moth-like against the sheen of silver.

There is no music. There is only the telling of the story.

Jesus ties a towel around his waist. Jesus bends with a basin. Says "not all of you but some of you." Says "do this later to one another." Then the garden and silver-wet coins in dry air. A severed ear in the dirt. The sweet curl of skin at the top of the ear. Then the heat of a charcoal fire on Peter's palms.

"No," says Peter. "No, no, no." Then Pilate and Jesus alone in a room, Pilate's voice a sieve and Jesus' voice a blade. Jesus says "everyone who belongs to the truth listens to my voice" and Pilate says "what is truth?" And then Pilate knows that Jesus is a map. He tries to release Jesus but the Jews cry for his death. And then Pilate knows that you cannot choose to be nowhere on a map. You have to be somewhere. Then he hands Jesus over to them to be crucified.

One of the readers coughs. One forgets it's his turn and has to be nudged in the dark. The person reading Pilate is also the person reading Peter. Jesus has the voice of a woman. It goes on and on. There is not much fidgeting in the audience. Winter-silt settles in the unplumbed depths of us. The depths where only naked skeleton fish float by, eyes bulging.

Then Jesus is nailed to the cross. Then the soldiers finger his tunic. Then a knot of three women shudders at the base of the cross. Then sour wine and the texture of sponge against his tongue. Then his body taken down and wrapped in myrrh and aloe and linen. Then the tomb. Then the knot of women unravels into threads of blackness that go tearing down the hills.

The story ends. No music. The stripping of the altar.

Kent takes the Bible and leaves. Miriam folds one scarlet runner and Heidi the other. The candles go, blown out and then disappeared. Finally the cross, grown dull without the mad-flickering of light upon it, is carried away. Then there is just stone and sand.

We depart in silence. And for once, we don't jolt back into our usual selves as we leave Koinonia. The sky is too dark and deep for even the most hideous sea creature to appear.

On Good Friday it arrives. A thick acceptance letter from the University of Montana. They want me. They want me to come and sit with other students around a large oak table and talk about poems. They want me to walk down clean hallways and perch beside a mentor while she draws dark diagonals through my poems to indicate new line breaks. They want me to drink beer in a bar beside the Clark Fork River. They want me thinking about the ugliness of a white "M" attached to the side of a mountain. They want me to eat brains and eggs at the Oxford Saloon. They want me to fall in love with men who lobby for environmental legislation and make jalapeño bear meat poppers and whistle for canines they call Brown Dog and Hound. They want me to read Elizabeth Bishop and Bashō and Tranströmer and Stevens. They want me inside Bernice's Bakery at 4 a.m., croissant dough draped over my forearms. They want me pounding out iambs and trochees on the sidewalks of Orange and Higgins. They think that I am good enough. They want me.

In the pinball machine of my heart, the silver ball is sliding through every shoot perfectly, is causing every light to go ballistic, every bell to electrocute the air with sound. I am certain the joy in my body is audible. I tuck the letter into my pocket and walk out of the dining hall and over to the large expanse between Chalet Hill and the dining hall, known in the summer as the village green and in the winter as the village white.

My Fiery Furnace group, gathered in the snow, looks like a tableau of the disinherited. Glimpsing a new life, however momentarily, makes me see this one afresh: dirty winter coats, poorly crocheted hats, pale faces, brittle hair. Eric is attempting to imbed a giant wooden picture frame into the snow. Andrew, wearing a threadbare cape from the costume shop over his windbreaker, is climbing the stone wall that encloses the outdoor Jacuzzi. He keeps slipping down or catching the cape on snaggled branches of ivy. My mother is covering a milk crate with snow so that Stella will have a pedestal on which to pose. Stella, beside her, is practicing Madonna "vogue" postures, six inches of gold lamé visible between the tops of her boots and the bottom of her coat.

In order to reach them, I have to step off the carefully tamped down path. I post hole immediately, up to both thighs in a snow the consistency of concrete featuring an icy crust on top. Also, I remember, Jesus is dead. We are supposed to be sad. This is tomb time for real. I try to take a step but succeed only in ripping my sock out of my boot and falling face-first into the wet snow. A dull dinging sound follows my fall. Michael, sitting in a lawn chair in the snow, holds up a silver mixing bowl in one hand and a wooden spoon in the other.

"Sackbut," says Michael, grinning.

The rest of the rehearsal progresses in a similar fashion. We have a script, but no characters. My mom and I ultimately volunteer to be Shadrach and Meschach. Michael is a disgruntled Abednego. But we are short a Son of God look-alike, the one who is supposed to appear in the furnace beside us. We try to convince Eric, but he claims he'll be too busy managing the flames.

As if to prove this, he lights a fuse connected to the wooden picture frame. A tiny wisp of smoke follows a soft fizzing sound. Then silence.

"This is going to be pretty lame if we don't have a fire," says Stella.

"I'll get it," says Eric, "I'll get it."

"Let's try this one more time," says my mother.

From the edge of the Jacuzzi, Andrew begins, "It is my will, as King of Babylon, that my people bow down to the golden image I have built." He gestures to the pedestal. Stella lifts her hands in the air to show off the length of her golden form, then turns slightly to the side and puts both hands on her knees a la Betty Boop, then turns her posterior to the audience and looks seductively over her right shoulder.

"Anytime you hear the sound of the cornet," (Andrew pauses and Michael blows a kazoo) "the flute," (Michael toots a recorder) "harp" (Michael strums prop ukulele from luau-themed party last month) "sackbut" (wooden spoon and bowl) "and dulcimer" (Michael shakes a gourd rattle) "you shall bow down and worship my—"

And then Andrew disappears because he has fallen backwards into the Jacuzzi. Because Andrew is sensitive, we try to muffle our laughter; we are not successful.

By the time I make it back to my room, the letter is damp. I take the white sheets out of the envelope and lay them side by side below my radiator to dry.

The Vigil begins between the school and the village Center; we gather around a pile of dry branches, trying to mark the shape of the thin stalks of wood against the softer darkness of the night.

A voice: "God said let there be light," and there is a scuffling sound from above us, on a balcony of the village Center, a scuffling and then a flicker and then a ball of flame, barreling through the air toward us, a ball of flame landing in the branches at our feet. A whooshing sound as the ball dissolves into the wider stretch of the branches and then lifts upward, the fire narrowing its fingers into the sky. I had seen Gregory and Eric working on the zip-line the day before, had seen them attaching a ball made of newspaper and tinder, had heard them cursing about weight and speed. The materials had looked flimsy and unpredictable so I was prepared to be underwhelmed. But the darkness hides the shabby construction—instead there is only the fire and the tail-chasing terror that comes from seeing a ball of flames come sailing toward you through the sky.

We leave the bonfire, lead by a villager carrying a single tapered candle. The kids scuttle ahead and we whisper and adjust our scarves. As we enter the V.C., we each take a candle out of a wooden box. These are Vigil candles, the kind with the cardboard skirt, the kind used mostly for "Silent Night" at Christmas. The pews have been pushed to the edges of the room and we stand in a circle in the heatless dark, listening to Callista sing about baptism and the coming of light. She bends, finally, and ignites the candle of the person beside her and the flame goes all the way around our misshapen circle until we become an imperfect and wavering ring of light.

Then we move to the Lift and hear the story of the Ark. Noah wears a yellow rain slicker and galoshes and the animals chortle and cackle and roar and paw at us from the loft area. We walk to the loading dock and witness Abraham consider sacrificing Isaac. Isaac stretches out on a board balanced between two sawhorses and Abraham is full of blustery gusto and arm waving, as though preparing to perform a magic trick.

I slip away and up the sawdusted stairs to the dining hall. Lucas is putting skewers of chicken into the oven and Kent is fiddling with the gears of a chocolate fondue fountain.

"How is it?" mumbles Kent around the screw between his teeth.

"It's good, actually," I say, a little surprised by my own sincerity, "too bad you guys have to miss so much of it."

"Not really," says Lucas.

Miriam looks up from a platter of chocolate-covered strawberries. "My turn?"

"Your turn," I say.

"Get out of here," says Kent.

Miriam leaves quickly, without bothering with coat and hat. I make a glass of peppermint tea and watch out the window as she skitters down the steps in her kitchen clogs, pausing only momentarily to turn toward the loading dock and to note the very real kitchen knife suspended over Isaac's outstretched body. Then she slides down the road to the village Center, hugging the cold to her chest.

When I slip inside the V.C. I don't see Miriam, I don't see much of anything. Villagers are gathered along the south wall, gazing at the piles of blankets scattered across the dusty floor. I hear Miriam's voice, coming from somewhere above me, speaking in the voice of the prophet Ezekiel:

> Then the hand of the Lord came upon me and set me in the middle
> of a valley full of dry bones. The Lord said to me, "Prophesy to

these bones." The Lord told me to tell the bones "I will make breath enter you, bones. I will attach tendons to you and make flesh and skin come upon you and you will live."

There is a shaking, a rattling. Maracas, I'm sure, but in silence and darkness, maracas are not filled with beans or seeds but human toe bones and teeth. The piles of blankets start to rise off the floor, swaying and shivering.

> Come breath, from the four winds, and breathe into these people that they may live.

And the figures drop their coverings and we see that they are bodies, arms and legs, torsos curving right and left, heads dipping like ladles toward an unknown source. And they begin to dance. Not a choreographed number but haphazard movements, leaps like jabs, hands pawing the air for purchase.

> And the breath came into them and they lived.

And I know it's Miriam's voice saying the words, and I know it's Finn and Kaia and Hallie and Maggie and Bethany out there dancing, but they are somehow not themselves. They are somehow a part of a story that continues, always, on the other side of us.

Everyone arrives, finally, at our set in the snow. And everything about our skit is different in the dark. Andrew's voice takes on authority, Stella (captured in my mother's flashlight beam) gleams gold and otherworldly. Michael hits every fake instrument note exactly and garners laughs from the audience. The fire starts and the flames stutter around the outside of the frame until the whole thing is lit and burning. My mother and Michael and I squeeze together so that from the path, where the villagers stand, we will look contained in a furnace heated seven times more than it was wont to be heated. Stella, still dressed in her golden idol costume, joins us as the Son of God figure, a move that likely theologically negates the whole endeavor, but oh well, we have four bodies where they should be.

I try to look through the frame, to the villagers on the other side, but I can't see anything. The glare of the flames makes it impossible to see beyond them. It's unlikely, then, that the villagers can see us. The furnace is a window stained with light.

I skip the story of Exodus and the lesson about getting your heart of stone replaced with one of flesh to indulge in a cup of hot cocoa in the dining hall. The overhead lights are off now and swaths of white fabric hang in loose folds from the ceiling. White Christmas lights wrapped around the exposed pipes illuminate the trays of food on banquet tables below. I steal a piece of gouda and savor the taste of smoke in my mouth. When I see everyone processing back down the road to Koinonia, I join them. It's midnight.

We gather in the entryway of Koinonia, just outside the doors of the Fireside Room. One of the doors is closed. The other is half-covered by thick wool blankets, leaving a tunnel to crawl through at the floor. This is the tomb. From inside, the sound of drums, not the sharp rap of snare drums but the soft thud of bongos. We wait silently for our turn to enter, exhausted but expectant.

Finally, it's my turn. I crawl from the dim, silent entryway into color and sound. The fireside ring is heaped with flowers: irises and lilies, peonies and tulips and flats of pansies and marigolds. Purple and pink and red and yellow. The colors obscure the sand and the stones so that, momentarily, it looks like a jungle has grown up in the midst of the circle of chairs. The deep violet linens on the triptych have been replaced with white and every colorful swath of fabric, every wall hanging or scarf, has been woven through the balcony railings or draped from the ceiling. Pastor Ben, clad in an alb and a stole streaked with gold, rocks side to side to the beat of the drums. And the villagers who have entered before me, the ones who have filled in the captain's chairs already, they are smiling. Unanimously they are smiling a joy that comes not from someone saying "Jesus is risen," not from the satisfaction of a certain story, but from crawling through six months of dimness into a room cackling with color.

I take my place in front of a chair. I join in clapping to the rhythm of the drums and I turn to watch the remaining villagers crawl into the room. More powerful than feeling the shock in my own body is watching the change, that's the only word I can come up with, cross the faces of my fellow villagers. I am watching them cross over.

Births and deaths, weddings and baptisms, graduations and retirement parties. These are ceremonies because they mark a line, between a past and a future, and we gather to watch the person move from one way of being in the world to another. More often, though, we are lost in the muddle, in the middle parts of life that contain no way to move from one territory to the next, no ceremony to leave behind a dream or an old love, no ceremony to mark the movement from healthy person to cancer patient, from employed to unemployed, from married to divorced. We feel these shifts as acutely but we have no ceremony to guide us across, and sometimes the steps of healing or awareness, of coming into knowledge or leaving hope behind, happen so incrementally that it would be impossible to choose a particular place or moment to mark the change.

That's why we are practicing resurrection. That's why I'm crying as I watch the faces of my fellow villagers change. Right now I am getting to see it happen, that movement across, the movement I'm longing for in my own life. I am remembering that it can and it will and it does happen, this coming into a new life, that our hearts change, but gradually.

I had forgotten flowers. I had not imagined they could come to this place. But here they are.

A Cut, a Climb, and a Café in California

I wake the next morning with the taste of resurrection still in my mouth. The movement forward and through last night, the crossing over (albeit briefly) still feels powerful and I'm determined to keep up the momentum—or, at the very least, the posture of momentum.

When I get to the dining hall for breakfast I note the leftover Easter eggs in silver bowls, blotched with odd stains from where they have lain too long against one another and dotted with drops of perspiration conjured by the warmth of the room meeting the slick coolness of the shells. I squint my eyes and focus on the cheery smears of color; I pretend a cold hardboiled egg on the tongue is the same as a warm one, that the place where pink dye pressed against purple and turned brown is lovely in its own way. On my paper napkin, I attempt to create a mosaic of the shells.

But the truth is that today is gray. Again. The toaster is broken and salt is dandruffing my wool sweater. The color of the yolk boiled too long, that gangrene hue, makes me want to gag. The shells don't remind me of a mosaic but the remnants of a technicolor house decimated by a storm.

Miriam saunters over as I take my first sip of coffee. The grapefruit she's peeling looks like an important prop against the backdrop of her black clothing.

"I need cheering up," I say.

"Been outside yet?" she asks, adding a curl of soft peel to my pile of shells.

"Of course," I say, "I'm here, aren't I?"

"Been outside by Koinonia?" she asks, her eyebrows scooting a belt-notch higher on her forehead.

I scoot back my chair and saunter over to the south end of the dining hall where the windows face Koinonia.

"Holy crap." Someone or ones have painted the snow.

The design is simple in nature. The fifteen-foot-high banks that flank the main door to Koinonia and run the length of the building, fifty feet in each direction, have been divided into four sections. The right side features hot pink above yellow and the left features green above blue. It's not paint, really. More likely food coloring diluted with water and spritzed, tirelessly, across the entire expanse.

"Jeremy and Lucas?" I ask.

"Happy April Fool's Day," says Miriam, splitting off a few sections of grapefruit with her thumbnail. She hands them to me and strolls back to work. The tartness works its way along the sides of my tongue and settles at the back of my throat. The snow looks awful. The smooth rise of the banks is now mottled by the footsteps of those who had to distribute the color equally to all parts. As the days grow warmer and the snow melts, the colors will bleed into one another. The piles will shrink and hunch into themselves and the whole thing will look like a child's art project gone horribly wrong. A variety of community members will be pissed by how it looks and will cover their disdain with an environmental complaint. It does look awful. I feel much cheerier.

And maybe this is why I'm not such a terrific Christian: I want my eggs white and my snow dyed. My cynicism always seems to suffocate my piety. Though I crave transcendence and sincere transformation, I'm capable of engaging in these sorts of experiences for all of five minutes. The part of me that aches as she hears the passion story is always at odds with the part of me that wants to tell the joke about Jesus on the cross (he calls to Peter numerous times, mumbling incoherently. Finally Peter climbs a ladder to he can hear his savior's final words and Jesus says, "I can see your house from here"). I don't know if this is simply the human condition (we can only feel sad for so long; then we need to turn and mock the sadness so that we can go on living) or if it is a personal failure, an inability to truly be vulnerable to something, a desire to protect myself, always, a little. This is the part of me that's afraid all Christians are on *Candid Camera*, that religion is a ruse, that I will be publicly exposed. The fact that Easter this year rolls directly into April Fool's Day feels like my internal predicament turned into calendar form.

But cynicism breeds its own kind of passivity. The kind that wants to sit, slouched on the couch, waiting for someone to prove the existence of God. Wendell Berry, in a poem oft-quoted in the village, talks about *practicing* resurrection. Or rather, his admonition to practice resurrection ends the poem, preceded by a list of activities that might or might not be examples of this ("work for nothing," "plant sequoias," "ask questions that have no answers," etc.). Maybe the winter has lulled me into such a state of passivity that I keep waiting for resurrection to find me instead of learning how to practice it. Since I'm a twenty-three-year-old woman instead of a sixty-five-year-old farmer-environmentalist I decide that, rather than beginning with dirt and sequoias, I will begin my resurrecting a little closer to home.

The Intended thought my hair was sexy, once upon a time, and so I grew it out. And, as Aaron mentioned to me many months ago, when I actually wash and brush my hair it is lovely—long and thick and blonde. What better way to prove to myself that I am finished, I am beyond, I have crossed over, I have begun anew, than to chop off all my hair. Or most of it.

Prior to arriving at Holden, Stella tried her hand at salon work. Trained at Aveda and practiced in the arts of the scalp massage and the essential oil, Stella is now the only one in the village anyone will trust with their hair. She is also incredibly artistic and incapable of completing most tasks without the use of glitter; it migrates from her artwork to her eyelids to her cleavage. Because Stella works part-time in the laundry and part-time in the bathroom-sized post office, we often find specks of glitter sparking our sheets or jazzing up the return address labels.

I climb to the second floor of lodge six to Stella' room. Her door features two photos: Jimi Hendrix (glitter puff-paint threaded through his hair) and the Dalai Lama. Below the Dalai Lama's perfectly lotused legs blooms an elaborately decorated toadstool. In a thought bubble above the Dalai Lama's head, careful script declares, "I have to poop!" When Stella opens the door she notices the thought bubble, rolls her eyes, and rips it down. There are two single beds in her room. One features rumpled sheets.

The other is strewn with colored pencils and glue sticks, with tubes of glitter and quarter-sized erasers shaped like flowers and fish. Stella spreads a plastic tarp on the floor and puts on Bob Marley. Then she turns her attention to me.

"Sister! What are you thinking?" she says, holding up a few strands of my hair to check for split ends.

"I think to about here," I say, gesturing vaguely to the space above my shoulders and below my chin.

"Mmmm hhmmmm," says Stella, pulling my hair behind my head until part of it bobs just below my chin. "I can see it," she says, satisfied.

"This is a good idea, right?"

"I love that you're doing this. This is such a good choice for you. This is such a good way to say fuck you. Fuck you to all of them, right? I am OVER men right now. I am over them. I'm so tired of the bullshit. Right?"

"Amen," I say.

"The only one who didn't just totally fuck me over is Johnny. Maybe I would hook up with Johnny again."

"Johnny the Ranger?"

"Yeah. I stayed in his bus once. In Twisp. I think it was Twisp. After a show."

"Is he the one who runs barefoot through the village?"

"Yeeeesssss!!! He's studying at Western, I think. No, wait, Evergreen."

"The school where you make your own major?"

"Mmmm-hmmmm. He's doing his on mushrooms."

"Mushrooms?"

"Mushrooms in the woods. You know, which ones are safe to eat and which ones are trippy and which ones are good for medicine. I think he hung out with Native Americans for a semester."

"Mushrooms?"

"How fucking cool is that?"

"Pretty cool," I admit.

"Yeah, Johnny's pretty cool." We both stare at our reflections in the mirror. Stella runs her fingers through my hair, lifting it up high above my head. "This will be intense," she says.

And she means it. For all of Stella's glitter and excessive enthusiasm, she's deeply intuitive about people and has a fine-tuned bullshit detector. When she couldn't make it on salon work she found a job as an entertainment director at a nursing home. To the geriatric community, I'm sure,

Stella was an angel. With sequins and shine and enthusiasm pushing out of her pores, she is always a healthy dose of life-well-lived.

Stella is quiet while she cuts. Bob Marley sings "Redemption Song" and I close my eyes, the shears like bird wings slicing into sky. When she finishes my head is lighter and twists more easily on my neck, but I don't look different. Not really. My hair has been the same color, parted in the same place, since fifth grade. The only thing that I've ever changed is the length and the only thing I've succeeded in doing today is cutting off one of the few things I thought might help to bring my Intended back. The truth, of course, is not that I want his disinterest, the truth is I want my own, want to think of him and feel only a subtle internal shrug.

"Do you want the hair?" asks Stella.

"The hair?" I say.

"Yeah. You know, to burn or something."

I can feel Sincere Me fighting Sarcastic Me for the answer. Sincerity wins. "Maybe I could throw it off the porch?"

"Yeah. That would be powerful."

And I think maybe it would be powerful. We gather up the corners of the tarp so that hair slides together into a pile, eight inches of it, the pain of the past knit into the strands. I pick up the pile. Stella holds the door for me and we clomp out onto the second story porch. I'll scatter it, like ashes, the hairs sparkling in the emerging sunlight. And then birds will come and build their nests and in that way the pain of my past will be transformed into new life.

Except that when I throw the ball over the balcony, the strands don't separate, they stay packed together and the whole clump lands in the snow just to the right of the lodge.

"Oh shit," says Stella, "that looks like something a cougar would cough up."

It does. It looks like a disgusting hairball—because, in fact, it is. And I look like a more homely version of my former self. So much for resurrection.

Even though the hair renewal plan was less than successful, I resolve not to revert to passive wallowing in the swamps of inertia. So when Miriam and Aaron invite me to climb Martin's Ridge with them the following Saturday, I accept. Martin's Ridge rises up directly behind the village; we won't necessarily climb to the top, just as high as we can scramble and still feel relatively safe. The day is gray, the snow slightly wet. We pack water, sandwiches of hummus and green pepper and cheese, emergency blankets, a first aid kit, and extra Smart Wool socks. We strap sleeping pads to the outsides of our packs to keep us dry when we rest. Our athletic wear has been worn so many times that even when clean, the scent of sweat is unmistakable in the armpits, along the center of the back. There is no trail, even when the mountain isn't covered in snow, so our way is marked by the thickest branches, the widest clefts in the rock. We stagger ourselves as we climb so if one of us kicks loose rock or shale or ice, the debris won't hit the person below. After climbing for forty minutes we stop and turn to face the valley. The village is the size of my gloved hand, the tailings a gash of orange in the drear. Railroad Creek isn't visible but we hear the bell, calling the other villagers to lunch.

Two summers ago I scrambled up the ridge with my Intended, overnight pack strapped to my back, the sky so cloudless it looked scoured. By the time we reached the top I was dehydrated, sun-stroked, sobbing not because I felt like shit but because of the way, the whole afternoon, the top of the ridge kept retreating. My eyes were so sunburned that I didn't want to admire the view, I wanted the inside of a tent and the cool of my own forearm across my face. The next day we hiked along the spine of the ridge, space falling away from us on either side, until we came to Cloudy Peak and a slope of scree and ice. He taught me how to sidestep down, foot parallel to the mountain, how to force the step so my foot could find purchase. I fell anyway and began to slide, ice against my belly and cheek. He grabbed the top of my pack. He saved my life.

I can't count on Miriam and Aaron to save me. They would. They could. But they aren't watching me the way a lover does. This realization is both liberating and exhausting. I am my own protector, I must trust my own capabilities, but this means I must be acutely aware of everything: my center of balance, the security of the alder branch above my head, the stones shifting below the boots of the scramblers above me. My main relationship, at this particular moment in time, is to the mountain itself. I need to pay attention to the land because no one is paying attention to me. And the land, this particular glaciated valley in the Cascade mountains, has its own story to tell.

The earth moves below us, but slowly. The earth below us moves at the rate that fingernails grow, a geologic fact that puts me in mind of the Sistine Chapel ceiling, Adam and God reaching toward one another, hands frozen but fingernails inching toward an embrace. Five hundred million years ago the oceanic plate was inching toward the continental plate. Far offshore, vents opened up in the water and minerals spewed up and settled and solidified around the vents. The plates crawled forward. Pressure built inside the rocks. The water eked away. Eventually, the hardened minerals got squeezed between the plates, pressed from prone to erect, from horizontal to vertical in the tectonic crush. The friction of the plates created lava and the lava flowed around those mineral deposits and made more mountains. Glaciers carved deep throughways. Now the layers of sediment and mineral run diagonally across Railroad Creek Valley. James H. Holden found one of these deposits on Copper Mountain, but the striations cut across the width of the valley. If we made it to the top of Martin's Ridge, we could track the same layers of sediment below our feet.

If it sounds confusing, it is. Geology manuals still use a topographic map of Railroad Creek Valley as an example of a complex glaciated valley. Minnesota geology is considerably simpler. If you want to see layers of sedimentary rock in Minnesota, you study the side of a cliff where some of the rock has been sheared away. Even grade schoolers learn how to count the layers, piling up horizontally like the mattresses that hid the princess's traitorous pea.

The geography, of course, suits Midwesterners, becomes us at a very deep level. In the Midwest, you have the feeling of things being below you, of history being buried. The older things live farther down and the newer ones are closer to our feet. In the Cascades it's different, two hundred million year old rocks beside two million year old rocks, the land a reminder of what happens when things collide, Glacier peak a reminder that rock still lives and moves, burns and worries. The peaks are jagged, yes, but there is a sense of sheer and jumble that goes deeper than that. Of raw exposure. The new isn't layered neatly on top of the old, the old rears up beside the new, jagged and toothy. I was born in Chicago, raised in Minneapolis. I know how to sugarcoat a sentence, how to brown breadcrumbs on a casserole. I order clothes from Eddie Bauer and L. L. Bean. I spend winters inventing new ways to say "gray sky" and "flat earth" and "eternal cold." But I've never been good at burial, at forgetting, at moving forward completely and directly. Though the mountains of Holden sometimes overwhelm me, sometimes feel foreign and claustrophobic, they are the geography of my heart.

But knowing the geologic story isn't the same as knowing the mountain, and though I'm trying to form a relationship, the mountain isn't as forthcoming as I'd like it to be. We've now reached a point where we can climb no higher (in my view) without ropes and harnesses or a shitload of testosterone and stupidity. So we unscrew the lids of our Nalgene bottles and eat a few M&M's. We snap pictures and rearrange the contents of our packs. Miriam is agile and athletic and her short-cropped hair looks sexy even when sweaty. Aaron's eyes look less hollow than they did back in November and his stubble looks intentionally rugged instead of unintentionally disheveled. I tell him he looks good. Better. I say it in the tone you use when you're trying to indicate that you're speaking both about a person's external and internal appearance. He nods. Studies me. Says I would look good too if I got rid of the pit stains and Walgreen's sunglasses. The truth is that both Miriam and Aaron could climb higher and that they possess the skills and courage to do so safely. I'm terrified and unsure whether my terror is a legitimate reflection of my capabilities or just cowardice.

As they suggest possible routes to the top I say casually "I'm kind of tired." Then, "It looks a little sketchy." Then, "It would be nice to have time to shower before dinner." Then, finally, "I don't think I can do it. I want to go back." They are kind about it and don't mock me as they could. And I feel only mildly humiliated until, for the first time, I turn my gaze down instead of up.

I had thought the descent would be easy, but the way down is not apparent. The way down is on the heels and ass, back pressed to the mountain, branches from elderberry and willow between the hands. Then Aaron suggests we slide down an avalanche chute on a sleeping pad. The avalanche danger is low but in no way is this safe, in no way am I myself when I agree. He sits behind and I sit in front and we pull the front of the pad up and he holds it so that I'm sandwiched inside. Then we begin to slide.

The air in my mouth and streaming from the corners of my lips, the heels of Aaron's boots sparking snow into my eyes, Miriam's distant laugh: this feels like love without love, my chest hollow and empty and waiting to be rung.

Somehow, even after the liberating ride down the mountain, the truth of Easter now seems false. The night of the Easter vigil felt so true to me: the stories, the mystery made possible by darkness, the sharp sweetness of flower and color and light. It felt like I had, like we all had, made it to the other side. Through the winter and depression and the stalled-out sick thunder of our own stories. But April doesn't feel as different from March as it should. My thoughts veer toward the Intended and then over toward my future in Montana. The refrain of a poem is followed by wondering whether he might step from the bus today, might just decide to appear and take me in his arms. Everyone would turn to see how right we looked together and no one would question this rightness. We would talk knowingly about the months behind us, a time of obstacles, a sprawl of cactus and coyote we had to cross so that we could arrive here, at the real, true ending of the story.

How can I, after all these months, after all this grief, still be thinking these stupid thoughts? After prayer and Reiki, after meditating about the tomb and getting drunk, after writing poems about Pompeii and tracing another man's ribcage with my index finger, after applying and getting accepted into a new future, don't I deserve to have my Intended exorcised from my thoughts? I read Gary Snyder and try to pretend that I, too, am looking at this relationship in retrospect, that I have enough distance to understand it:

> We had what the others
> All crave and seek for;
> We left it behind at nineteen.

> I feel ancient, as though I had
> Lived many lives.

> And may never now know
> If I am a fool
> Or have done what my
> karma demands.

I feel ancient too. Because the truth is that I don't know how to let go of this particular story.

In mid-April I fly with my family to California. What could feel more like resurrection than spring break in California? We stay at my uncle's beach-front condo: white wicker furniture, paintings gobbed with magenta and turquoise sunsets, beige carpet striated by vacuum cleaner marks all the way to the edges of the room. On the deck that overlooks the Pacific is a telescope. I fit the quarter-sized lens into the socket of my right eye, then turn the dial so that the sea blurs and sharpens, until I can count the seals sunning themselves on a rock a quarter-mile offshore, until I can distinguish the rubbery backs of dolphins rising through the staid metal surface of the water.

We spend one day hunched over tide pools. It is nice to be a benevolent onlooker, hovering over a tiny community, watching the organisms go about their business. The tentacles of the anemones have the softness of a throat but stick briefly to the tips of my fingers. I observe a hermit crab for a long time, his scuttle from rock wall to a tiny stand of kelp, the tide lifting him occasionally as though the forces of gravity have been swayed away. Then the pool looks foreign, lunar, and I bring my fingers to my lips to taste the earthy sting of salt.

We eat avocado and bacon, drink iced tea and margaritas and Diet Coke. In the late afternoons, when the sun scorches the deck, I lay on a plastic deck chair in one of my mother's old hippie bikinis, listening to Bob Dylan and Jack Johnson on my Diskman. I train my eyes on the horizon, let my breath come warm and easy. The sea is a landscape that shows all its cards, so different from the mountains that perpetually hide the view of what happens next.

California is not Eden either, of course. As I sit in the café in town, my notebook open and pen at the ready, women strut by in tans not acquired via the sun, coral and turquoise necklaces hanging between their perfectly rounded breasts. They wear high heels with their capris; their bulging handbags feature silver chains for straps. Behind their sunglasses, mascara and eyeliner make their eyes doe-like but heavy, as though a certain kind of endurance is required just to keep their lashes afloat. Even as they sip cappuccinos at the table beside me, their cup rims remain perfectly white, lipstick strangely affixed to their lips.

By contrast, I have not yet shed my five extra pounds of winter fat. My skin is ghostly, legs unshaved. My body is unused to the temperature (warm in the sun, cool in the shade) and by the time I finish the mile-long walk from the condo to town I sport crescent-shaped stains below my arms and hairs dark with sweat along my temple. In the shade, I shiver. The California women are reptilian, sweatless in the sun and content baring cleavage in the shade. Even as I inwardly roll my eyes in disgust, I know I'm being unfair, grouping them together into a single category of superficial blandness in much the same way guests group the Holden staff into a box labeled "hearty." But my limited time here doesn't permit me the complexity of a different kind of vision.

Nevertheless, being around these people makes me feel slightly ill. There is an insistence here on the external—the hair, the legs, the face, the clothes, the handbag, the car—that is mildly terrifying. Beauty and polish makes an object easier to hold, but what happens when cancer bloats the skin, when grief carves hollows below the eyes, when childbirth widens the hips and loosens the belly? On the other hand, at Holden we seem to circle intensely around the inner self. There is no chance to feign or pose or preen. We are stuck being ourselves all the time. And though I would choose this option in a heartbeat over the superficiality here, I am tired of living honestly with others. Tired of the lack of anonymity, tired of sharing every meal with at least one person I've hurt, one person who annoys me, and one person who will eat more than her share of the chocolate cake.

I am hoping Missoula will be a middle way. A community of writers to depend on but coffee shops and restaurants where I will recognize no one. More fashion than Holden but an outdoor sexiness preferred by cowboys and forestry grad students. Mountains low enough to climb in tennis shoes in a few hours. An airport. A thrift store. Croissants. Missoula won't be Eden but maybe it will be damn close.

We fly back to Seattle and drive to Wenatchee to spend the night before the ferry ride in the morning. From a pay phone near the hotel, I call Natalie, a village friend who lives in Seattle. I tell her about the village, about California, about my future at the University of Montana. I try to keep my voice light, positive, assertive, and confident about my new path. Natalie has ties to the Intended and I'm hoping she'll pass along the tone of my voice in addition to the details of my future.

"Oh shit," she says.

"What?" I say.

The pause is long enough that I wonder if she's hung up the phone.

"I don't really want to be the one to tell you this."

"What?" I say. The receiver is oily beneath my chin and I move it farther away from my lips, as though this will soften the blow.

"Saul is moving there too," she says quietly.

"Where?"

"Missoula."

"With her?"

"With her," says Natalie. "He got a job at the co-op."

"At one of the co-ops?"

"At the only co-op."

"Oh," I say. Because what else is there to say.

I wear my sunglasses on the boat the next day. I wear them at the dock and on the bus, though the sky is gray and the lenses make the world impossibly dim. Hearing Natalie say the word reminds me. His name is Saul. He is a human being, complete with his own flaws and his own future. For all of my intentions otherwise, he is not my Eden.

His name is Saul. He is a person. And I miss him.

Vespers tonight is Prayer around the Cross. When I enter the room is dark. Wooden boxes filled with gritty sand sit on the stones of the fireside ring. Beside each box, a handful of thin white candles and on the floor in front of each box, a pillow for kneeling. In the middle of the fire ring rests a Guatemalan cross, made of squares that feature bright tableaus of Jesus healing, teaching, and dying. Maggie, our boarding student, plays a simple tune on the piano; her face, illuminated by the music light, is a bright spot in the room. I take a seat in the second row of captain's chairs and, because the room is chilly, I don't take off my coat, just hunker down farther into it.

Ben, the pastor and Forrest's father, welcomes us. He invites us, when the music begins, to participate in singing or humming the simple chants. He invites us to come and kneel and light a candle. If we kneel at the box at the foot of the cross, others will come and pray with us. Otherwise, we will be left alone.

"The light shines in the darkness," says Ben, striking a match.

"And the darkness has not overcome it," we reply.

Maggie plays and Miriam leads us in the first chant: "Take oh take me as I am / summon out what I shall be / set your seal upon my heart / and live in me." Forrest is the first to approach the candles, dragging his father behind him. He hops up onto the fireside ring itself and crouches next to the box in his sleeper pajamas. Light flickers across his pale face. He lights one candle and grinds it into the sand. He goes for another candle and Ben stops his hand, folding it into his own larger fist while bending to whisper in Forrest's ear. The foot-bottoms of the pajamas are textured and appear, from this distance, amphibious. Forrest tries to wrench his hand free and Ben lifts him off the fire ring and carries his thin four-year-old body back to its seat.

Heidi kneels and so does Heather. Miriam segues into a different chant: "Nothing can trouble / nothing can frighten / those who seek God shall never go wanting / nothing can trouble / nothing can frighten / God alone fills us." Aaron kneels and I take the cushion across from him, at the foot of the cross, at the place I have avoided all year, at the place where I will not be left alone with my failures.

I light a candle and close my eyes and they come. Two strong hands on my shoulders. One on my head. Someone kneels beside me and I feel a hand on my lower back. A few fingers on my spine, a palm on my shoulder blade. It is warmth and power and presence. It is a gathering behind me that I feel but cannot turn to see. My grief comes and they catch it. Whether you call it God or not, it is a force, this knob of people gathered around me. They are not anonymous; I can smell wet wool and body odor, patchouli and bleach and the lasagna we had for dinner. I feel their breath, their bodies shifting into more comfortable positions as time goes on. They are not anonymous but because I cannot see who, exactly, is loving me at this moment, I cannot respond to this love as daughter or friend or lover or colleague or teacher. The only way I have to respond at all is by receiving what they have to offer. I kneel for a long time.

MAY

The Cost of Hospitality

Think of Penelope's loneliness. Twenty years of waiting for Odysseus to return. Think of the quiet of the first years. Rooms filled with cold sunshine, fields going green and gold and black. Think of the long length of her dining room table. How she sometimes thought of it as a boat, she at the helm, with no one to row her anywhere. She hated the solitude, longed for company. Then one day, the suitors arrived. One hundred of them. Obnoxious, loud, oblivious to the rhythms of her house. *This kind of company is worse than loneliness* she thought to herself as she wove the shroud she would soon unravel.

So it is in the village when, every weekend in May, 150 high school students descend upon us. The kids come from California and Oregon and Washington, members of church youth groups excited for a chance to roam untethered in the mountains. There will be one chaperone for every seven students and two students for every villager. We will be outnumbered.

Theoretically, we should be prepared for this outnumbering. During the last weekend in April we transitioned the village back to its summer self. We opened guest rooms, we brought the adirondack chairs out from hibernation, we replaced the ping pong table and foosball table and comfy couches and chairs in the dining hall with the heavy rectangular tables on the south end and the circular tables along the middle. I helped bring the Tree of Life back to fruition and now it stands proudly, dangling its rusty

95

and unappetizing fruit. We should be ready for the arrival of 150 high school students but I, for one, am not.

Now that I know Saul will be haunting the streets of my new life, Missoula no longer seems quite as appealing as it did a few weeks ago. Of course I still want to go, but part of the initial appeal of Missoula was that the experience of it would be mine, untainted by the presence of my family or troubling figures from the past. I have never actually been to Missoula; in my mind it looms like one of Calvino's invisible cities, only instead of being populated by melon vendors and bickering gods and bearded women, the Missoula of my imagination is filled with mulleted bartenders and wizened poets and men clad in lumberjack shirts and Chaco sandals. My imaginary city has been punctured with the realness of Saul, by the complexity of my feelings for him, by the ordinariness of my own past heaved into a metropolis that was supposed to contain only my future. Simultaneously, Holden is beginning to take on its robust, summertime, secluded-village-among-gorgeous-peaks appeal. Whereas a few months ago, opportunities for chats and hikes, performances and parties stretched interminably into the horizon, now the end looms close and I want to keep the staggering beauty of spring and my final intimacies with this community to myself. I am not ready to share any of it with 150 anonymous high schoolers.

Specifically, I am feeling decidedly not ready right now, during the Wednesday community meeting. I've assumed my usual position, prone on the balcony of the Fireside Room, chin cupped in hands, surveying the room. To my left, Lucas leans against the wall, out of the sight line of those downstairs, writing a letter on Holden stationary. Jeremy sleeps beneath his felt hat. Below, Miriam holds up a clipboard. "I need extra pancake flippers on Saturday," she says.

Finn holds up another clipboard. "We need help sweeping the village Center and moving the pews."

Ben, the pastor, holds up another. "Communion assistants," he says.

"We're opening up the pool hall and snack bar," says Heidi. "The kids and chaperones will scoop the ice cream and monitor the bowling but we need community members on hand in case there are any questions."

As the pass-arounds circulate, we are also admonished to set a good example, to welcome the bus, to smile, to interact, to appear approachable. I roll my eyes. Lucas nibbles at a cuticle, Jeremy dangles one of the clipboards (one to which no one in the balcony has added his name) above the heads of those below. Aaron grabs it and sets it on the fire ring next to the other clipboards, the other clipboards that also feature only a few signatures. Not nearly enough signatures.

There is a steely silence in the room. Janet, one of the directors, stands and clears her throat. "You know," she says, "it has been a good winter. Sometimes a hard winter, but a good winter. And we've lived together, this group of us, for such a long time that it's not surprising that the village feels like ours. Feels like it belongs to us." Janet is wearing a faded Holden Village sweatshirt and jeans. Her hair is held back from her face with a thick cloth headband and then cinched at the back of her neck with a ponytail holder. Out of the last twenty years of Janet's life, ten have been spent at Holden. She folds her hands in front of her. "But this place belongs as much to each of those May youth weekenders as it does to any of us. The work of the place is hospitality." She looks up toward the balcony. "The work of this place is renewal for all. You have spent the winter cooking meals, and scrubbing floors, and installing sprinkler systems—and that's all well and good. But your real work begins now. To do all of these things in the service of others who come to this place in need. That's what you signed up for."

And so we sign up. And so, on Friday, we all gather to greet the bus. We've been encouraged to dress in tie-dye clothing, in part to appear colorful and in part to play into Holden's hippie commune stereotype. I'm wearing a tie-dye sarong from Ecuador like a cape. My mother sports a shirt with poisonous frogs navigating psychedelic swirls; she waves toilet bowl brushes around like an airport traffic controller. Someone has brought over instruments from the Fireside Room. While Lucas and a few others start up a drum circle, Finn gyrates his hips, banging on a cowbell as hard as he can. Danielle, Natalie, and Johanna, the elementary girls, perform a hula routine and Forrest and Tasha scamper around, pawing the air with the tie-dye socks over their hands.

As they emerge from the bus, about 30 percent of the high schoolers immediately intuit the flavor of the village. These students break into genuine, cheek-stretching smiles, and a couple even shimmy their hips or do little hand jives as they step down. The other 70 percent do not intuit the flavor of the village. Their facial expressions range from fake smiles (pressed lips and flared nostrils) to doe-eyed shock, to unfettered disdain. One girl, after taking in the wild exuberance of our performance, freezes in place and turns to the girl on the step immediately behind her as though she might be able to slip back on the bus and head for a Starbucks.

As promised, we welcome. We guide them to the dining hall. We point to the drawings of the lodges on their little welcome maps and then point to the corresponding buildings. I reassure one girl wearing a t-shirt that says "Jesus Loves Me" that there is indeed shampoo for sale in the Holden store. We sit with our new guests at lunchtime. We show them how to scrape their plates, we point out the coffee urns and the small reach-in refrigerator where the milk is stored. While I demonstrate the function of a tea strainer, I see one boy lingering beside the center island, lifting each condiment like a specimen. I feel like I should do a formal introduction: "Boy with Mariners hat, meet brewer's yeast; brewer's yeast, meet boy in Mariner's hat." Even though it's overwhelming, to suddenly have this many bodies in the dining hall, I feel an immediate affection for these high schoolers. They seem so confused and woebegone, so very much like acne-covered sheep. And I am glad to feel useful, glad to be the shepherd, glad to feel knowledgeable.

This feeling of satisfaction lasts approximately six hours. By dinnertime, they've figured out the place. All 150 of them. They know where the coffee is, where the bell is. They're acquainted with the Craft Cave and the village Center and the pool hall. And we've made them feel so welcome; we've repeated so often that the village is theirs, that they believe it. Any building, any nook or cranny they haven't investigated, they feel comfortable discovering. After dinner, I find three of them sitting on the porch swing of my chalet. Two girls flank a boy who looks especially smug. The boy's legs are long enough that he can push against the porch railing with the stub of his Adidas shoe. As I approach I hear Girl #1 say, "I'm freezing."

"Get in here," says the boy jovially, spreading his arms along the back of the swing so that both girls can snuggle into his armpits.

"Much better," says Girl #2.

"Hey," says boy, noticing me.

"Hey," say the girls.

"Hey," I say.

"Do you live here?" asks the boy.

"Yep," I say.

"All year?" asks Girl #2.

"Yep," I say.

"Cool," says the boy.

And then I open the door and enter my chalet. Their presence on my porch isn't against the rules, exactly. But during the winter—and even during the summer—chalets are treated like houses. The common areas—the porches, the kitchen, the living room—are used solely by the residents of the chalet. The porch isn't mine *per se*, but I certainly don't offer them a drink. I don't tell them to stay as long as they'd like. And I definitely do not join them.

When I wake the next morning, I realize it's not just the presence of so many more bodies in the village that overwhelms, it's also the increased decibel level that's an affront: dozens of feet crunching down the gravel road, voices calling "wait up" or "I'll meet you down there" or "where's Robbie?" or "did you get my fleece?" A soccer ball thuds against the side of Lodge Three and from the porch outside the snack bar I can hear three female voices practicing a tremulous version of "One Tin Soldier" for the talent show tonight. The creek is loud with snowmelt and the birds are zealous in their tweeting. It's only 8:00 am. I decide to skip breakfast.

Somehow, we make it through the first weekend. On Sunday, just after lunch, all 150 bodies pile back on the buses. They've only been here forty-eight hours and they've mostly interacted with one another, so unlike with the J-Term students, there is no flurry of e-mail and address exchanges as they depart. There are tears. Whether the tears have to do with a transformational experience or what that bitch Cindy said at the campfire last night is unclear; likely it's a combination of both. Either way, the bus doors slide closed and the tires kick up dust and we wave and wave until the vehicle disappears. The quiet is sudden and eerie.

Though most of the snow has melted, there are still piles below the eaves of the larger buildings, a result of the accumulation of roofalanches. The students were, of course, delighted by these piles, by the novelty of a snowball fight in May. I am struck not by the sight of the piles but by their continued effect on the air. Walking down the road, slipping from sunlight into shade, passing dry ground and then snow drifts, I move into and through pockets of warm air and then cool. The body in one zone and then another. The same road but this stretch a different experience from this one, this length a different quality of bright, a different potency.

May will be like this, I know now. The taste of summer, the bustle and anonymity, here and then gone. Presence and then absence. What will be and what is. The contrast makes me appreciate the weekdays more, makes me savor the thirty-five days I have left before I am the one getting onto the bus, before I am the one who will disappear.

Tailings

On Monday, Christine asks me to assist Forrest and Tasha, the kindergarteners, with an ongoing project: we are to record the progress of Spring.
Forrest and Tasha are each given a clipboard with a simple worksheet attached. I carry their pencils. We exit the school and walk fifty feet to the
alder tree beside the pool hall. I lift them, one at a time, to see the branches.
Then they kneel in the dust in their jeans and set about replicating the
branches inside a white square on the worksheet.

"No leaves yet," says Forrest.

"Not yet," says Tasha, "but buds."

"I want to touch the buds," says Forrest.

I lift him.

"They're soft!" he proclaims.

"Exactly," I say.

"Exactly," Tasha repeats without looking up from her drawing.

Forrest leans toward the bud with his lips slightly parted.

"But not for eating," I say, lowering him gently.

"Some plants are for eating," says Tasha.

"That's true," I say.

"But not this one," says Forrest.

"Not this one," I say.

The branches on their worksheets are spindles, are rivers going nowhere, are witch fingers with buds for knuckles. Forrest makes a mistake
and erases until he rips a hole in the paper. I am afraid he will dissolve in
frustration but he touches the edge of the frayed paper gently instead.

"It's soft," he says, "like a bud."

"Yes," I say.

"Exactly," says Tasha.

When they are satisfied with their renderings we repeat the process up
at the Ark, where they document the progress of a few pointed iris stalks.
We look for the snowshoe hare to see if his coat has changed color but
succeed only in terrorizing a number of chipmunks. Then we head down
the road, holding hands, our destination the covered bridge where we will
record the water line and draw pictures of the exposed boulders.

On our way down the road, we spot a doe and two fawns making their
way up from the creek. There aren't yet leaves to block all of the light so
our path is dappled with both sunlight and shade—and for the first time I
understand the markings on the backs of the fawns, how from above they
blend perfectly into a spring morning. Tasha and Forrest and I go still. The

doe sees us, then turns her head so that just one eye is upon us. Then she continues across the road, stepping carefully, a young woman testing the waters, skirts hitched to her thighs. The fawns are skittish but not deliberate. They dally behind their mother and then cross the road, start-stopping as they remember and then forget and then remember our presence.

Deer are not an anomaly in the village, they are perpetual summer guests, but there is something about this particular encounter that feels miraculous. The rush of the creek beside the emptied silence of the village, the clean light and the smell of warm wood and earth and dust. The doe isn't dangerous, though she could be if we threatened her fawns, but I feel, for one of the first times in my life, suddenly protective of the two beings flanking me, both deep responsibility and also an awareness of their awe.

A year before our breakup, Saul and I spent part of the summer at Holden. It was June and we were about to set off on a two-night camping excursion. I'd done a little hiking at this point but the longest I'd ever been out was one night so doubling my record felt mildly heroic. Our packs were heavy, towering things. I'd packed each item carefully, granola bars and water and gorp and raincoat within easy access, sleeping bags and fleece pants and cooking stove secured more deeply in order to keep my center of gravity low. I always liked the way I looked setting out for these excursions: tan, thin legs plugged into wool socks and relatively clean hiking boots, baby blue bandana wrapped around my head with blonde braids dangling on either side. And Saul looked magnificent: curly brown hair, wide smile, powerful biceps and thighs and competence—in these situations he radiated confidence. I would have followed him anywhere.

We set off down the road. Our packs were still heavy towering things but now they were strapped to our backs. We were no longer agile, no longer light on our feet. We were mules. We were strong. We were moving forward.

At the outskirts of the village, a baby chipmunk ran directly under Saul's foot. If we hadn't been burdened with the packs, maybe he could have sidestepped. Maybe not. The baby chipmunk was dead. Crushed entirely. And so was Saul. All those little bones gone to nothing under his foot. The feel of death in the sole of his boot. The animal body suddenly not a body anymore.

He took off his pack. He made sure the animal was dead, that it wasn't suffering. He found some work gloves and moved it off the road, below a bush. Then we sat on a low stone wall with our packs beside us and he put the heels of his palms to his eyes. I rubbed his back, told him it wasn't his fault, that there wasn't anything he could do.

Then we put our packs back on and started hiking. But it wasn't the same. There was this tiny dead thing between us, too small to truly grieve and too disturbing to forget. We bickered instead. Nit-picked. Made each other miserable. Nine miles is a long way to hike with a forty-pound pack if you're not used to hiking with a forty-pound pack. The whole way, as I whined, he promised it would be worth it once we reached Lyman Lake. He described its turquoise stillness, the massive glacier that would hang as backdrop. Except that it was June and the snow was still abundant. At one point we had to abandon the trail and cross a boulder field instead. And when we arrived, Lyman Lake was covered in snow. Not beautiful, fresh winter snow but dull-around-the-edges Spring snow. We had arrived at a barren wasteland. The wind picked up the cold on the lake and whipped it around my body.

I was pissed. But I loved Saul too much to realize that my sadness and anger had nothing to do with the carcass of a baby chipmunk or the Antarctic vista in front of us. It was the ending of our story, felt but not known, present but unspeakable.

A few days after we returned from the hike, Saul left me a note: "I hope you always find what you need throughout your days and your life and have the insight and courage to know what that is." He was able to articulate what I couldn't, loved me enough to give me the permission to let him go. It took another year before I was able to wrangle that kind of courage. And it has taken most of this year for me to forgive myself for doing so.

I enjoy the rest of the week and suffer awkwardly through another May youth weekend. The following Wednesday, Christine and I depart on a two-night camping trip with the elementary school girls, riding the bus down the road in the morning so that we can catch the boat on its way up lake to the town on the northernmost tip, Stehekin. Like Holden, Stehekin features a small winter community that caters to an influx of summer guests. But unlike Holden, Stehekin is not an intentional community but a resort community that holds intentional events from time to time during the winter so that folks can stay social and sane. Stehekin features a hotel with a restaurant, lakefront rental cottages, a school, an orchard, and a top-notch bakery.

We march off the boat and straggle to a campsite about two hundred yards away. After we set up our camp we rendezvous with a ranger who takes us on an educational tour: the orchard, a waterfall, and finally a site where a few other rangers are setting up a prescribed burn.

The ranger is slim and soft spoken. He has long, straight brown hair that he's tucked neatly under a baseball hat. He walks us over to a tree that he pats as though it's a long-lost friend. "This is a ponderosa pine," he says. We instinctively look up to see how high the trunk travels into the air before becoming muffled by branches. "This guy loves a good fire," says the ranger, running his thumb along a jigsaw of bark. Johanna looks at him suspiciously. Danielle pulls her braid from under her backpack strap and begins rebraiding it. Natalie stares at the ranger, unblinking, inflating a violet gum bubble to the size of a large orange. The ranger tries again. "Sometimes we think of fires as bad, but fires actually help this tree. It's only when the cones get really, really hot that they release their seeds. It's called pyriscence."

"So fire doesn't kill the tree?" asks Johanna.

"Well, it's possible. It all depends on temperatures and levels of moisture and nutrients. But even if the tree died, it would have released thousands of seeds just before dying. And many of those seeds would fall on soil made even more rich and fertile because of the fire."

"So *most* of the trees die," says Natalie.

"No, no. Many of them survive because they have such great bark." The ranger pats the tree proudly again. "The bark acts as an insulator and keeps the core of the tree from getting too hot. And it smells good."

"Like what?" says Danielle, looking up from her braid.

"Like vanilla or butterscotch," says the ranger. The girls exchange expressions of mild disbelief. I feel a little skeptical myself.

"Give him a try," says the ranger, stepping back from the tree so that all of us can step closer.

And we do. Natalie and Johanna and Danielle and I gather around the tree and insert the tips of our noses into crevices between the outer layers of bark. At first all I smell is the scent of warm wood and Natalie's grape gum but then I breathe deeper and there it is. Butterscotch. And not a vague, nature-version of butterscotch but a full-bodied, treacle-sweet scent. I am reminded of Strawberry Shortcake dolls and scratch-n-sniff stickers. It is like stumbling upon the witch's candy house in the middle of the forest.

Except the sweetness is inside the tree and as soon as I step back an inch, the experience dissolves entirely.

"That's cool," says Johanna.

"Yeah," says Danielle.

Natalie nods her assent around the purple bubble covering half her face.

The ranger steers us over to a field where two other rangers are clearing brush. "They're preparing for a prescribed burn," says our ranger, tucking a stray strand of hair back under his cap. "They're clearing the perimeter to make sure the fire doesn't spread."

Johanna narrows her eyes at him. "How can you do that?"

"We're careful. We've done this a lot. We contain it. The prescribed burns help to prevent bigger and more devastating fires that could endanger people or homes. Fires are nature's way of clearing things out, starting over. Does that make more sense?"

"I guess."

"How do you put it out?" asks Danielle.

"Well, it pretty much puts itself out."

"What if it doesn't?" asks Natalie.

"We only do these burns in the Springtime, when the chance of regular forest fire is low and most of the trees and plants have a lot of water in their systems. It's almost impossible for the fire to spread."

"Almost?" asks Danielle.

The ranger tightens the straps on his pack. He's not really a natural speaker and he's not great with kids. He's clearly an eighteen-year-old boy who likes to walk through the woods and got stuck with the educational gig. Danielle and Natalie and Johanna have been living in the village for three, four, and six years respectively. They've heard countless fire alarms, been lectured in fire evacuation procedures. They know fire as dangerous and unpredictable and they are understandably skeptical about the idea of fire as controlled cleanser and promoter of new growth. The pause lengthens. The ranger fixes his gaze just above Danielle's head. Natalie blows another bubble. Johanna crosses her arms in front of her chest.

"Well," says the ranger. "The thing is—studies have shown. And we've done this a lot. A lot. And I can just guarantee there just, there won't be a problem."

"You know what?" says Christine, "let's talk about this more back at our campsite."

The ranger lets out a sigh. Johanna shrugs. Natalie sucks the bubble back into her mouth. The girls turn away and begin the slow walk back, their packs bobbing and bumping as they lose their footing and then find it again against one another.

Back at the campsite, I sleep in a tent by myself for the first time in my life. The girls share a different tent and Christine, who is Outdoorswoman Extraordinaire, uses a single person bivvy sack. Because our campsite is twenty yards from Stehekin's single road, the quiet is punctuated by both the occasional sound of a car engine and the rustling of animals in the douglas firs surrounding us. After about half an hour the giggling of the girls gives way to the light snoring of one of them. The extra space in the tent feels depressing so I pull my pack in beside me, a move that seems pathetic now but hopefully will feel comforting to my half-conscious self when she half-wakes, feels a presence beside her, and then sleeps again.

I turn the dial on my headlamp and center a book in the ring of light: a volume of poetry by Louise Glück called *Meadowlands*, a retelling of the Odyssey, the poems set sometimes in a contemporary world, sometimes in an ancient one. Tonight I'm transfixed by a poem called "Penelope's Song." Glück's Penelope sends her soul to climb a spruce tree to wait for Odysseus' return. She instructs her soul to sing, to be generous, to shake the boughs of the tree in greeting. Glück's writing is so deft that by the end of the poem I almost forget it's not Penelope herself who is playing the role of patient wife: it's her soul we see, the location of her body remains undisclosed. Like much of Glück's poetry, the beauty of Penelope's speech veils a river of venom, a hatred caressed into twenty-four lines. I understand this kind of hospitality.

The next afternoon we take the boat down lake to a site called Prince Creek. We go on a short hike through a recently burned area. We learn to identify miner's lettuce and stick our noses in a few more ponderosa pines. In the evening, while Christine and I get a fire started, the girls spend forty-five minutes trying to throw a rope over a tree branch so that we can hoist our food out of the reach of bears. The following morning, as the boat nears, I notice the 150 high school students on board, the bodies among which we will be ferried back to our home. I take a deep breath and try to appear hospitable.

"Hospitality" is one of those words within the Christian vocabulary that is lovely in theory and irritating in practice. Hospitality is great if you have a large and spacious house, a guest bedroom, and a maid. Hospitality is fabulous if you are an extrovert or your guest is an introvert. Hospitality is easy if your guest is eager to be helpful and magically intuits how to load your dishwasher, when to be quiet during *Law and Order*, and when to take a long walk by him or herself. Because I am an impatient introvert who takes episodes of *Law and Order* very seriously, I am not very good at hospitality in the outside world. At Holden the practice of hospitality is even harder work; we are not just opening our home to a passing traveler, we are insisting that our home *is* the home of the traveler. And because Holden is also the home of the stranger, we who reside there are (theoretically) equally in need of welcome, equally hungry for hospitality.

All the same, I want the high schoolers off the boat. I at least want them to stop talking. To comfort myself, I purchase a warmed (well, microwaved) cinnamon roll and cup of coffee from the tiny galley café. I manage to find a metal folding chair next to a group of girls huddled around a spiral notebook. The girl who holds the notebook rattles off three names and then turns to face a friend with stringy brown hair, glasses, and a shirt that says "Sassy" in silver letters.

"I'd marry James. I'd kiss Dylan. And I'd—" she looks over her shoulder and then breathes the next words furtively "fuck Stephen."

"You'd fuck Stephen?" says girl with notebook.

"Shut up!" says Sassy.

"Stephen? Seriously?"

"Shut up seriously."

I turn away from the girls and face a group of boys who are taking turns flicking one another in the ear as hard as they can. I slip off my Chaco sandals and try to concentrate on the warmth of the coffee cup, cradled between my bare feet, then on the sandpaper-sweet of the cinnamon I lick off my fingers. Then I notice the only person on the boat who seems to be more annoyed than I am: James.

James arrived at the village for the first time in the summer of 1998 and 70 percent of the village was mildly terrified. James is a middle-aged white man who looks like a retired gangster and speaks like an Old Testament prophet. He wears baggy athletic shorts, a white wife-beater, and a skin-tight black do-rag tied savagely around his head. His sideburns edge the corners of his mouth and the jangling of gold chains around his neck betrays his scuttling approach. James exhibits the perpetual mumble of an unmedicated homeless man and if you stand near him long enough you can catch the threads of his thought: Armageddon and the wrath of God mixed in with complaints about the behavior of the guests in Lodge Three, room fifteen. It's actually not the phrases that are uncomfortable so much as the inflection, the sentences stilted and gruff, the words of a Forrest Gump steeped in the book of Revelation.

That first summer James was assigned to housekeeping. My mother was the head housekeeper and luckily she has always specialized in rehabilitating those who are damaged or wounded in some way. She assigned James the task of vacuuming the lodge hallways and emptying the trash from the lodge bathrooms. James completed these tasks with a precision and fervor that many of us found deeply unsettling.

Vespers proved even more uncomfortable. At the beginning of each evening summer service, when the village Center is filled with the bodies of four-hundred-plus people, the names of the people who have arrived that day are read aloud. The new villagers stand as their names are announced and when the last name is finally uttered, the rest of the community applauds enthusiastically. At this point James would rush from the roon, fingers in his ears, mumbling something loudly about "the inconSIDerate people who clap without THINKing, who are RUDE, not very THOUGHTful." When the applause ceased he would stalk back into the room, usually between the front row of pews and the altar, and find his seat again.

I am not particularly good with people who are damaged or wounded in some way. I understand that Jesus lurks in these sorts of people, that these are good moments to overcome my own misconceptions and fear. I also understand that saying things like "these sorts of people" and assuming that their differences from me constitute "damage" or "wounding" is condescending and ignorant. The Jesus message is, after all, that we are all broken and wounded in some way and that claiming some kind of emotional or spiritual health is the surest sign of illness. Nevertheless, the truth is that I initially found James quite annoying. One typical afternoon, as my mom and I stood in the sun, laundry baskets on our hips, eyeing the lemon bars set out for coffee break, James came shuffling up to us, stopping to linger about a foot from my mother's elbow. His glance was quick: her face, the pavement, the mountains, her face, his belly, her face, the pavement.

"Hi James," I said.

"Hi James," said my mother. "Do you need something?"

"ArmaGEDdon," said James. "Nine-one-one," said James. "ArmaGED-don nine-one-ONE." My mother nodded encouragingly. I mumbled something about needing to refill my sanitizer bottle and walked briskly away.

The next summer James brought with him a navy winter hat named Tuque. Tuque is a French-Canadian word for "hat" and also the proper name of this hat. Tuque accompanied James everywhere. He rested on James' left thigh during Vespers, he lay on the shelf of the cleaning closet while James vacuumed. In addition to Old Testament doomsday prophecy, James now had a whole new lexicon. "Awwwww, Tuque!" he would say, holding the hat up to show random villagers. "Tuuuuuque," said James, drawing the first syllable into a lullaby. His approach to Tuque was gentle, nurturing. He knew where Tuque was at all times. Other villagers began to noticeably relax around James. They developed an affection for Tuque. They asked after Tuque. When Tuque was presented they knew to stroke gently the polyester weave of the hat.

The following summer, Tuquette appeared. My mother sewed baby Tuques out of pink felt. Tuque carried Tuquette and the babies inside himself. At Vespers, when I asked James about the babies he would peel back the layers Tuque and Tuquette to show me. "Shhhhhhh," he would say, "they're sleeping." Then James would smile.

Now, three years later, though his appearance hasn't changed much (I can see the high schoolers eyeing him warily), James is a welcome sight to me. As he plugs his ears and cringes at the decibel level in the boat, as he mumbles under his breath and darts out the door onto the deck, I entirely empathize and wish vaguely that I could feel comfortable externalizing my own frustrations in the same way.

The boys on my right side have decided to direct their flicking skills toward a tightly folded triangular piece of paper instead of one another's ears. One with acne highlighting his cheekbones like blush holds up his hands, thumbs touching, index fingers vertical. Another boy, wearing a shirt that says "Rugby Players Do It Without Protection" flicks the paper between the other boy's fingers and yells, "Field goal!"

"Nice," I say, trying to look appreciative.

The boys pretend to ignore me but Rugby-shirt ducks his head and the other boy's acne brightens considerably.

May high school crowds aren't the only groups Holden hosts. During the summer and early fall, aspiring pastors, gay pastors, single women, lay people who care about ecological liturgy, retired prostitutes, homeless men, homeless women who sing, and amateur improv troupes all rotate through the dining hall and hot tub, the lodge porches and the teaching sessions. Most groups come for a week. The first few days they are awkward, uncomfortable, anxious. By the end of the week, the group isn't a noticeable group, they have integrated enough to simply become a part of the community. In the summer of 1999, my mother was "buddied" with Eileen, a former prostitute from Chicago. They went on walks, ate ice cream at the snack bar, saved seats for one another at Vespers. (Eight years later, my mother will attend Eileen's wedding. Three years after the wedding, Eileen will fact-check my mother's young adult novel about a young would-be ballerina who moves to Chicago and becomes a stripper instead.)

But hospitality at Holden only goes so far. Though we welcome people who are wounded and hurting and in transition, Holden also adheres to the laws of the world outside the village. Staff members sign a covenant before arriving: we agree to adhere to worldly law (no pot, no underage drinking, no stealing, no sexual harassment) and also village law (mandatory attendance at Vespers, shifts on dishteam and garbology, thirty-six hours of work every week). Because there is no actual law enforcement present in the village, the sole punishment is the NBO: Next Boat Out. Long before *Survivor* showed up on syndicated television, long before contestants on national TV were voted off the island, Holden directors were voting people off the mountain.

Stories of folks who have been NBOed vary from comical to tragic. A group of teenagers caught playing naked pool were sent packing. A potter in residence who left clay fingerprints on the thighs of sixteen-year-olds had to go. A few were asked to leave in the midst of winter when it became clear that the depth of their depression was more than the spiritual practices of the village could plumb. Over the course of a certain summer, the appearance of a teepee out by the ballpark and a volunteer with a suitcase full of Ecstasy resulted in the expulsion of quite a few members of the community.

While I understand the practice (and while I certainly consumed enough beer as a teen in the village to deserve to be NBOed), I find it painful too. Maybe it is too reminiscent of Adam and Eve, trudging their way out of Eden below the length of a fiery sword. I know that Holden doesn't have the resources to help some of the people who pass through the place. We don't have psychologists or psychiatrists on hand; serious rehabilitation of any sort is not what we're set up to do. Nor does anyone want Railroad Creek valley to become enveloped in a haze of pot smoke. And yet. By some standards we are a perfect community: fresh food, meaningful work, spiritual practices, environmental beauty galore. And some people find deep healing here. Some find a way to cross over. So why not everyone? And if we can't offer respite and transformation to the most broken, then where on earth do we expect it to happen? Is the problem ultimately that some people are too wounded to be healed by paradise? Or does Holden not contain enough of the rest of the world to be useful in the way it could be?

Maybe the most difficult part of hospitality is that underneath the term is the nagging question: to whom will you deny entry? In college I read a brief essay by Immanuel Kant called "On a Supposed Right to Lie Because of Philanthropic Concerns." I don't remember much of the essay, just the central dilemma: if a murderer comes knocking on the door to your home, the home in which you are harboring the murderer's intended victim, do you let him in? For Kant the situation is about lying. About how even in this situation you shouldn't say, "No one's here. Just making some biscuits. Playing a little solitaire." You shouldn't lie because duty, what's right, should always prevail. You shouldn't lie because maybe your untruth prompts the murderer to go around to the back, where maybe the murderer finds your hideaway sneaking out the window. Had you told the murderer the truth, your friend might have been saved. Because you can't predict the events or the outcome, you can only, at any given moment, do the right thing.

I can't help thinking about Kant's invented scenario as a litmus test for hospitality instead of honesty. The worst possible stranger arrives at your door and you are called to let him pass over the threshold, to let him splay his dirty boots on your antique trunk, to let him consume the very last of your Thin Mints.

The May youth weekenders are a significant step up from Nazis but still—hospitality is exhausting. By the end of the month of May, I am beginning to miss my fellow villagers. It's suddenly clear that we are nearing the end of our time together, that soon our tapestry will begin unraveling. Some of us will stay for another year and some will go and some will go and return and go and return, drifting through the village for years to come. But this particular constellation of people, this village, will never be the same again. After feeling motionless, static, impotent for months, this movement forward feels sudden and abrupt. I feel like a mother who, after nine months of perfecting the art of waiting, is suddenly sent home with a baby. Here is the new life we've all been waiting for—but now we have to figure out what the hell to do with it.

At the very end of the month, I join forces with Jeshua (bookstore manager and resident folk musician) and we put together an evening of poetry and music. Most of the village comes. They gather in the Fireside Room. Jeshua slides a circular board over the fire ring to make a stage. A single spotlight illuminates us as we take turns moving in and out of its circumference.

Jeshua plays a song about working in the bookstore. I read two poems. Jeshua sings a song about how Marv, the garbologist, looks like Terry, the busdriver. I read two poems. Jeshua sings a song about how all of his songs use the same four chords. Then I read my last poem, my favorite of the year. I like writing in the guise of other people and after reading *Meadowlands* I wanted to try my hand at Penelope. But I can't seem to get inside her head. It's Calypso I'm drawn to, the sexy nymph who keeps Odysseus captive for seven years. But when I try to write her seductively, I can't, her story only comes out sad. I'm wearing a dress Saul made for me. It's floor-length. The color of the ocean when seen from above, when recognized from a distance. Along the bottom part of the fabric, are tiny cutouts, triangles and diamonds. The dress fits me perfectly; Saul knew my body and he made it that way. I read:

> Keeping a man excited on an island for seven years
> is not an easy task.
> The tricks of lovemaking are hard to stretch out
> over the long slow looping moons of many months.
>
> Even breasts are hard to keep interesting.
> Believe me, I tried.
> Coated mine in shells and sand,
> let them surface seductively
> between waves of salty brine.
>
> But here is how it is with men:
> There is always another ship on the horizon.
> Even during lovemaking their eyes are squinting slightly
> as though the next bark into shore
> might lie behind the iris of your eyes.
>
> Odysseus left on a raft he made from bark
> and leaves and I'll tell you what:
> I was a little happy.
> When the purpose of your life
> is to make another love you,

you start to hate your own reflection.
Even your voice sounds traitorous,
words jump from your throat, unbidden, betraying who you are.

The only way to keep a man like that
is to build a boat yourself.
Put him in it while he sleeps. Send him out to sea.
Then, when he wakes, you have become the horizon,
the thin line of home and flesh
he unwillingly left behind.

In many ways, the whole story of the *Odyssey* is simply a succession of failed and successful attempts at hospitality. The idea of welcome was, of course, important to the Greeks long before it became a pet term in Christian circles. *Philoxenia*, as the Greeks called it, wasn't just common courtesy, wasn't just a dash of potpourri in a guest room, it was a social construct with strict rules and expectations. Paris's crime wasn't kidnapping *per se*, the Trojan War began because he broke the bond between guest and host (the fact that the broken bond involved the host's wife did not help matters).

This obsession with *philoxenia* wasn't born simply out of the goodness of the Greek heart; rather, it was tied to the presence of the gods among them, laced to real fears of retribution. Should the scraggly beggar to whom you denied entry turn out to be Zeus, you were screwed. This understanding isn't too distant from Christian belief. We're not (or most of us aren't) too worried about being smote by a disguised supernatural being, but we do welcome the stranger in part because we believe that divinity might linger within that person. Jesus claimed, famously, that we would find him within the person in need; Christians are called to feed, to clothe, to comfort, to welcome.

Still, I identify more with Glück's reticent and bitter Penelope; finding Jesus in the May youth weekenders is hard. Calypso, too, wasn't particularly good at hospitality, not because she wasn't capable of receiving and entertaining (she was actually rather good at the entertaining part) but because, when the time came, she wasn't graceful about letting her guest depart. She kept him longer than he wanted to stay. Maybe I'm drawn to Calypso because she widens the scope of *philoxenia*. We don't usually think of hospitality as romantic. We think of it as a relationship between host and guest, between known entity and stranger, between friend and friend. But maybe hospitality prepares us in a different way: to keep the doors of our hearts open, to let those we love pass in and out. To feed them while they're with us and then to let them go.

JUNE

The View from the Second Level

In ten days, I will leave the village. In ten days, I will climb on the bus and kneel on the green vinyl seat. I'll press together the sticky hinges on the window, slide it down, and press my head and neck through the narrow space. I'll accept a card from Christine, my name across the front in her careful script, I'll squeeze the hand Miriam offers me and let the elementary girls' fingertips graze my palm as they attempt airborne high fives. Lucas will raise his gaze from the skin of the drum he has locked between his knees. He'll nod and smile and I'll nod and smile and whatever was between us will be neatly sealed and flown away. A snowball will narrowly miss my head, thrown by Aaron who has somehow managed to find left-over snow in the skulky shadow of a building. My mom will cry and Finn and Adrianne will cry, because Vicky, one of the high school students, is leaving too. Michael will turn and shake his butt at me and Jeremy will tip his felt hat and everyone else will wave. The bus will hiss and lurch forward. A minute later all of it, the mountains and people, the road and the lodges, will be collected into the single frame of the rear window. Contained and retreating until finally all of it is consumed by the dust.

This will happen in ten days. Right now we're in the midst of a Wednesday community meeting and for the first time in many months I'm sitting in a captain's chair on the lower level of the Fireside Room instead of claiming my usual anonymous perch in the balcony. I'm waiting for my official long-term goodbye.

Holden staff who commit to living in the village for a full year (or, in my case, the school year) are considered long-term. Long-term staff receive perks like health insurance and a small monthly stipend. When long-term staff depart, they are given a bundle of white tapered candles and a pamphlet about readjusting to the world outside of Holden. The candles are to be lit in memory of one's year in community or just in moments of quiet prayer or meditation. Though they are always received with a certain amount of reverence, the candles often get misplaced over the course of the volunteer's transition to the outside world—only to reappear again months or years later buried at the bottom of a cardboard box or melted together in the trunk of a Toyota. While many former long-term staff members, when asked, report that they have no idea where their candles are, none of them can remember throwing them away.

The pamphlet contains words of wisdom for building community outside of the village. I'm lucky to be immediately entering a different sort of community, an academic program that, in spite of having zero religious affiliation, will by its nature demand that I see a certain group of people repeatedly over the next two years. Though we won't share our grief while praying around a cross, tears will indeed be shed over poems that tremble with a similar kind of vulnerability. But not everyone from my long-term community will have this good luck. Many villagers will face unemployment or, after all our talk of vocation, jobs that offer a paycheck but little else. Though all of us crave anonymity now, returning to a world in which we are, for the most part, unknown, might prove debilitating. After all, if you are unknown, your presence or absence hardly matters. While Holden has forced us to face the full burden of who we are, leaving Holden will force us to face the burden of who we're not. We're leaving the tide pool for the sea.

In addition to the candles and pamphlet, each long-term community member is also honored with a small speech by a member of the village who served as the departee's supervisor or mentor. Though Vicky and I aren't leaving for ten days, this is the last official community meeting of the winter. Summer staff will begin to trickle in, and next week we'll move to more practical and efficient staff meetings, consisting of announcements and pass-arounds, framed with first welcoming the new staff and then recognizing those who will be departing. No joys, frustrations, and concerns.

No consensus decision-making. Vicky and I both wanted our official good-byes to transpire while the last residue of our winter community is still intact.

Vicky and Diane, one of the directors, stand at the front of the room. Vicky wears a filmy, ankle-length brown dress with puckered embroidery across the bust line. Part Armenian and full-fledged hippie, Vicky piles her incredibly long brown hair into various looping formations on top of her head. She eschews shaving and as part of a senior art project completed a series of paintings of cave-flower-vagina hybrids. Vicky is a year older than any of the other high schoolers (our only graduate this year), but she also has more complex baggage from her past; both of these factors contribute to her seeming considerably older than the others, closer to a twenty-something volunteer than a high school student. She's also more effusive. When words simply cannot express the enthusiasm she feels, Vicky opens her mouth and mimes, with her hands, the rush of emotion pouring from her lips.

Diane, a hand on Vicky's shoulder, talks about Vicky's effusiveness, about her willingness to be vulnerable and speak the truth. She talks about Vicky's growth—who she was when she arrived and who she is now. She tells a funny anecdote and ends with a few words of blessing. We applaud. Wipe tears from the corners of our eyes.

Then it's Vicky's turn. She faces us. "All of you. This community. You know how much you have meant to me. Every last one of you. Even those of you I wasn't close to. You helped me. I'm a different person now. There are no words." Then she brings her hand to her lips and in the silence floats her gratitude out to all of us.

Then it's my turn. Christine and I stand and face the villagers and Christine begins to speak. I don't really register what she's saying. I know the words are kind. Complimentary. But they don't feel like enough. Partly this is because Christine, though sweet, is not as articulate a public orator as Diane. But mostly it is my own expectation; somehow I thought at this moment a whole version of myself would be offered up, jewel-like, to shimmer in the light. The rough spots would be made into unique complexities and the gifts I'd humbly neglected to remember would be buffed to blinding shine. I thought at this moment I would be given a version of myself I could forgive.

Ann Patchett talks about forgiveness in terms of writing. She writes about the failure she felt, over and over again, when the world she rendered on the page failed to live up to the one she had created, fully formed, in her head. She had to forgive herself, over and over again, for not being able to reconcile those two versions of a world.

So much of my own unremarkable suffering, I realize now, springs from my own inability to reconcile the life I want to lead, the person I want to become, with the life I am in and the person I truly am.

My imagined self moved on so seamlessly after the breakup. My imagined self remembers the Intended fondly but not obsessively. My imagined self grieves in quiet, patient ways and doesn't fall into bed with inappropriate men. Imagined self doesn't make the mistakes her parents made, doesn't still feel their divorce, at times, like a sliver to the heart. Imagined self is pious without being annoying. Faith flows through her like water. Imagined self is hospitable even to the person eating Doritos loudly during *Law and Order*. Imagined self didn't gain seven pounds over the winter. Imagined self aches to climb higher, trusts the mountain, trusts her own capabilities as the cougar ambles closer and closer and closer.

Which isn't to say that imagined self should be obliterated. Imagined self keeps me on my toes, keeps me leaning forward, keeps me trying to be better. Nevertheless, the gap looms large. While imagined self lingers in the ether, bathed in all her glory, I have to forgive myself, this self, for not being the protagonist I desire.

When Christine finishes her speech I hug her, accept my bundle of candles, and turn to face my fellow villagers. I had thought I would come up with something brilliant and funny and humble to tell them, thought I might reveal a profound truth or describe a hilarious anecdote. But I have nothing left to say. Except, of course, "Thank you."

Then I put my fingers to my lips and float all I cannot say back out to them.

Oddly, although the year has been filled with religious ritual, with Christian practices that help us mark the passage of time, the two final rituals of my year in the village are deeply secular: prom and graduation.

Because there are only five high school students, prom is not a regulated school event but a village celebration, organized by the high schoolers. I prepare for prom in my parents' chalet with Michael and three of the high school girls: Adrianne, Maggie, and Bethany. Adrianne and I are going traditional, using prom as an excuse to curl our hair and our eyelashes, to put on heels and slip on sheaths that cover only the narrow expanse from breastbone to knee. While we primp, I wear a pair of green hospital scrubs and a shirt with intricate lettering that reads *Fuck Your Fascist Beauty Standards.*

Maggie and Bethany, considerably less vain and considerably less patient with primping, have foraged gowns from the costume shop. Maggie's is a full-length poofy princess number in pale blue. Bethany's dress is also ankle-length but the fabric looks like something Pa Ingalls would have purchased for Laura by the yard. Bethany has taken the time to tie her three-inch long hair into fifteen small ponytails, giving herself a kind of hedgehog on the prairie look. Maggie lets me smear glitter and shadow on her lids but when I get to the liner her eyelid begins to quiver under the pencil, the thin pale skin like a bird heart gone frantic with terror.

At 7 p.m. my date arrives. Kent stands awkwardly in the doorway in a brown suit, bow tie untied and hanging loosely around his throat. In his hands he holds a potted philodendron.

"What's that?" I say, lifting a tendril of the plant.

"Your corsage," he says.

Finn, Adrianne's date, arrives next. His suit is impeccable and his tie matches her dress. He offers a bouquet of handpicked daisies and lilacs. Adrianne curtsies demurely.

Michael, date of both Maggie and Bethany, eventually emerges from his room in a thrift store tuxedo three sizes too big. His clip on tie is the size of a small partridge. With a little prodding, we convince my mother to put on her dress too—a slinky costume shop find in peacock blue, a rhinestone shimmering like a Cyclops eye at her waist.

We line up on the porch steps for pictures, all seven of us, each person on a separate step. My mother stands in the dirt road in front of the chalet to take the picture. The sky is the quiet blue of early dusk; after the photos we all take a moment to ogle the moon's crisp outline and mottled center.

Then Adrianne says, "I'm cold" and my mom says, "see you down there" and Peter says, "I'm going to need a little wine before we go" and I say, "bring a Nalgene with you" and Kent says "don't forget your corsage, dear" and so I break a tendril off the philodendron and let it drape casually over my shoulder. Adrianne and Finn lead the way down the road followed by Michael—Bethany on one arm and Maggie on the other—and then Kent and me. Strangely, we don't speak. There is simply the crunch of gravel below our feet, dust working its way between our toes, and the swallows swooping and darting, charting the contours of the valleys with their forms.

Three minutes later we arrive at Koinonia. After much consideration, the high schoolers chose the theme "Work It!" and now the words shine brightly through their inspired decorations. There are no balloons. In lieu of crepe paper there is yellow caution tape. The tape flutters in the doorways and hangs limply from the acoustic tiles in the slightly-more-appealing-than-a-bunker Creekside Room. On the tables around the outer edges of the room, the high schoolers have displayed various work implements: hammer, saw, wrench, screwdriver, a blender, unrecognizable mining implements, a geometry textbook, a lantern, work gloves, and a whistle. In the far right corner Lucas, dressed in the flowered green jeans he wore for Transition so many months ago, tinkers with an ancient stereo and an iPod. Just outside the room, in a nook usually reserved for the quiet contemplation of magazines, the high schoolers have hung a lawn blanket from the ceiling to create a photo station. To the top of the blanket they've affixed construction paper letters that spell out WORK IT. An African violet on a wooden stool and a fern on an old baptismal font frame the backdrop and create, of course, aesthetic appeal.

The whole village is there. We dance. And those who don't dance stand along the edges of the room and smile, occasionally picking up the work implements, occasionally swaying their hips a little if the tune is familiar or particularly compelling. I dance and my mom offers surreptitious sips of wine. I dance and then Heather and Stella and I pose for a photo, each of us holding an imaginary gun pointed in a different direction a la *Charlie's Angels*. Then Jeremy and I try for an awkward prom pose, both of us facing in the same direction, his arms wrapped around my waist to clasp my hands in front of me. Except when the camera clicks he grabs for my boobs instead.

We dance. Lucas plays the Rolling Stones and Ben Harper and Blondie. We shimmy and jump. Miriam lassos me with a boa. Finn mimes pushing a lawnmower. Michael jumps and jumps, grazing the ceiling tiles with his knuckles. Lucas plays "Tupelo Honey" and I miss Saul and then he plays "Send Me On My Way" and I don't. Like millions of teenagers around the world, we come to prom at a moment when a certain portion of our life is coming to an end. And so, along with millions of teenagers around the world, the people dancing around me blur into soft focus; nostalgia embroiders every song.

Suddenly it seems possible, physically, to go. To leave. And this makes us want to stay, swaying to a song we don't know or used to know or would someday like to remember.

The next week passes in a blur. I pack the three spiral-bound journals I've filled with poems this year. I pack the photo album. I pack the quotes I taped to my bulletin board and candles I didn't burn. I pack my snow pants and my fleece hat, my Smart Wool socks and my deceased grandmother's cocktail dress.

Miriam comes up for a last glass of wine. Dee Dee and I take a long walk down the road, mud thickening on our hiking boots. Lucas and I eat wasabi peas and listen to Jeff Buckley and page through old Sierra Trading Post catalogues. At school we all go through the motions. And then it's Friday.

Vicky is the one graduating senior this year so she gets to make all of the decisions regarding the graduation ceremony: the place, the speaker, the food we'll eat in celebration afterward. She decides she wants to accept her diploma on the second level tailings pile, wants folding chairs and a podium hauled up and arranged in a semi-circle so that she can graduate with a view up the valley and down and, more importantly, a view of the village where she's spent the last year of her life. She doesn't want to be in the village, she wants to be above it, wants perspective and scope.

The folding chairs are uncomfortable and the tailing dust is gritty under our feet. While we wait for everyone to gather, Forrest and Tasha use fist-sized rust-colored rocks to try to break open other rust-colored rocks. They are searching, they say, for gold.

Because a speaker system is useless on a mountain, much of what Miriam, Vicky's chosen speaker, says is lost in the wind and the high twisting white clouds. But I catch her advice to Vicky about creating a home:

"On the very first night in a new home, I invite people in. Friends if I have them nearby or the movers or my family members, though usually they're sweaty from lugging cardboard boxes and trunks up creaky flights of stairs. I share a meal with them. Most of the time it's pizza, because I haven't unpacked my kitchen supplies. And most of the time we sit on the floor because the chairs and couches have boxes on them. Or maybe I haven't been able to afford a couch. But when I share a meal with others, that's when I know a place is home."

And though I know what she's suggesting to Vicky has to do with the ritual of sharing food, of breaking bread together, what strikes me most is the decision itself. The calling out of a place as home as the main thing that makes it so. Not time lived there, not knowledge of the landscape, not the people who occupy the space with you, but the saying that it is so.

Vicky's estranged parents sit up by the podium beside her, a solid foot of empty space between their maroon folding chairs. About a hundred yards away from our gathering, amid a few scrubby trees that have actually taken root, is a pile of mining debris: bed frames, oil drums, rusted bolts and coffee cans. Mixed into the older trash are more contemporary items: a plastic press pot, an ice cream freezer, an exercise bike. Behind Miriam and Vicky and her parents, across the valley, Martin's Ridge hangs as a backdrop to the proceedings.

When I look up valley, the view is a mallet to the heart. Dumbell and North Star are all of the usual clichés: gray and rugged peaks shrouded in snow and skirted in shaggy green. There are wild idylls up valley, pristine and secluded, that remain untouched, unmarred by human hands. The view down valley is less dramatic. Though I can't see Lake Chelan from where I sit, the empty swath of sky (undivided by mountain peaks) indicates the open water below. Further down valley are stores and cinnamon rolls, speedboats carving impermanent white wakes into the blue. Down valley the world as it is and up valley the world both as it used to be and as we imagine it should be. But we have staked our claim here, on a pile of toxic residue, somewhere in between.

Holden is not Eden. It never will be. Eden, the future, the imagined self: these are places at which we never arrive. We remain, instead, hungry at the gates. But this hunger, this yearning, is powerful. The reach toward goodness—and more importantly the ways we buoy one another as we reach—this matters.

Tomorrow I will climb on the bus and watch the village disappear. I'll gaze out the dusty window, backpack on my lap, as the bus winds past alumroot and chicory, past lodgepole pine and silver fir. I will pass half-hearted waterfalls and abandoned vehicles and gaps in the bracken where lovers could slip, unnoticed, down to the creek. After ten miles the bus will stop and the driver will shift into a lower gear for the switchbacks. The lake will appear as a puddle, then a pond, then as an expanse of turquoise cold.

On the ferry I will stand on the back deck, the roar of the motor edging out thought until the sun and wind force me inside to rest. When the boat docks, Vicky and I will haul our suitcases and boxes up to Field's Point landing. Cars will slumber in patient rows; the asphalt will feel hard and slick below our feet. I've promised Vicky a ride to Seattle so she'll wedge herself into the passenger seat, my small stereo perched on her lap, a CD whirring out song after song into the air between us. Vicky and I, usually eager to chat, will not. Instead, we'll wait for the tears and the grief to come, the desire for catharsis edging our ribs as the car climbs higher and higher. But the catharsis won't come.

At the top of Snoqualmie Pass, the sky will open wider than we've seen in months, clouds flushed copper, the horizon spanning to the edges of our peripheral vision. And I will feel that same stretching inside myself.

I have spent almost a year in the village. I haven't been healed, haven't entirely moved on. But I've grown, within me, a greater capacity for all of it: suffering and joy, loss and forgiveness. Holden didn't let me escape the world; instead, the village helped me make more room for the world inside myself.

All of this will happen tomorrow. Right now, I'm in the hours before departure, in the space before leaving. The graduation crowd is dispersing. Aaron and Lucas and Jeremy toss a Frisbee around the pile of mine debris. My mom and Peter and Finn collect the folding chairs. Having rolled their pant legs and t-shirt sleeves up to better inhale the sun, Adrianne and Maggie and Bethany sprawl on a lawn blanket. Up by the podium, a small group gathers around Vicky; she touches the tassel of her mortarboard and grins. Kent and Miriam are already fading into the fringes of my vision, headed back to the village to put the final touches on a graduation feast.

I walk to the edge of the tailings pile and stand in the place where my mother photographed my father and me twenty years ago. The dust leaves streaks across my white socks. Below me, the buildings look like Monopoly pieces: the chalets snug and tidy, the lodges long and sturdy. In front of the buildings, parallel to the creek, the road appears and disappears between the trees, threading its way through the realm of what I can see.

Works Cited

Adams, Nigel B. *The Holden Mine: Discovery to Production,* 1896–1938. Wenatchee, WA: World Pub. Co. for Washington State Historical Society, 1981.

Bell, John L. "Take, Oh Take Me As I Am." Chicago: GIA, 1995.

Berry, Wendell. "Manifesto: The Mad Farmer Liberation Front." *The Mad Farmer Poems.* Washington, DC: Counterpoint, 2008.

The Bible. New Revised Standard Version. Minneapolis: Augsburg Fortress, 1990.

Buechner, Frederick. *Wishful Thinking: A Theological ABC.* New York: Harper & Row, 1973.

"History." *Holden Village.* http://www.holdenvillage.org/about-us/his/.

Hoagland, Tony. "Adam and Eve." *Donkey Gospel.* Minneapolis: Graywolf, 1998.

Johnson, Art, Jody White, and Dickey Huntamer. "Effects of Holden Mine on the Water, Sediments, and Benthic Invertebrates of Railroad Creek (Lake Chelan)." *Washington State Department of Ecology,* July, 1997.

Patchett, Ann. *This is the Story of a Happy Marriage.* New York: HarperCollins, 2013.

Snyder, Gary. "Four Poems for Robin." *The Back Country.* New York: New Directions, 1968.

Taize. "Nada Te Turbe / Nothing Can Trouble." Chicago: GIA, 1986.

Weil, Simone. *Waiting for God.* New York: Harper and Row, 1951.

Whitman, Walt. *Leaves of Grass.* New York: Random House, 2001.

Yoder, John Howard. *Body Politics: Five Practices of the Christian Community Before the Watching World.* Nashville: Disciple Resources, 1992.

———. "What Kind of Political Person Was Jesus and Why." Audiofile of a lecture by John Howard Yoder presented at Holden Village, Summer, 1978. http://audio.holdenvillage.org/node/3734.